Praise for *Cracking Complexity*

"The formula is a very fascinating, unique format – which as of today – is easily the best return on time and money I have ever experienced."

—Mike Crichton, Head of Asia Pacific, Middle East and Africa, Sandoz

"*Cracking Complexity* is the first book that takes on the daunting task of architecting a systematic approach to leveraging serendipity. Komlos and Benjamin detail the many scientific and sociological breakthroughs in addressing complexity to provide a compelling case for how organizations can tackle a future where the ability to simplify and manage complexity will be the crucible of success. Required reading for every CEO!"

—Tom Koulopoulos, Chairman, Delphi Group

"The formula is truly a breakthrough for engaging the organization in solving big challenges with speed and agility."

—Cathy Nash, CEO, Woodforest National Bank

"The formula created an inflection point for our company. We quickly won our people's hearts and minds for new levels of growth and performance."

—Bob Guillocheau, Chairman and CEO, Ascensus

"*Cracking Complexity: The Breakthrough Formula for Solving Just About Anything Fast.* Really?! Yes, REALLY! This formula has been used for some very complex issues by some very large companies. I think there will be a lot more of that now. But, I also see where this concept can be used for smaller complex problems. I plan to use it in my consulting business, and just in aspects of life."

—Dr. Mark Goulston

"Working with the Davids and using the techniques described in this book we transformed two of our businesses, one in Canada, the other in Europe, with outstanding results to our revenues and margins. Key to the approach is the involvement of staff in the process which for us really enhanced the quality, engagement and speed of implementation of our new strategy. I think anyone addressing complex business issues will find this book of immense value."

—Mark Jones, ex Company President and CEO of AstraZeneca Canada; President AstraZeneca UK and Global Vice President Southern Europe

Cracking Complexity

The Breakthrough Formula for Solving Just About Anything Fast

David Benjamin
and David Komlos

NICHOLAS BREALEY
PUBLISHING

BOSTON • LONDON

First published in 2019 by Nicholas Brealey Publishing
An imprint of John Murray Press

A Hachette UK company

24 23 22 21 20 19   2 3 4 5 6 7 8 9 10

A CIP catalogue record for this title is available from the British Library

Library of Congress Control Number: 2018959160

ISBN 978-1-473-68564-2
US eBook ISBN 978-1-473-68566-6
UK eBook ISBN 978-1-473-68565-9

Printed and bound in the United States of America

John Murray Press policy is to use papers that are natural, renewable, and recyclable products and made from wood grown in sustainable forests. The logging and manufacturing processes are expected to conform to the environmental regulations of the country of origin.

John Murray Press Ltd
Carmelite House
50 Victoria Embankment
London EC4Y 0DZ
Tel: 020 3122 6000

Nicholas Brealey Publishing
Hachette Book Group
53 State Street
Boston, MA 02109, USA
Tel: (617) 263 1834

www.nbuspublishing.com

Contents

Dedication

THE FOCUS OF *Cracking Complexity* and the Complexity Formula at its core is on groups, not individuals. But when it comes to changing the world, disrupting a market, fending off disruption, fixing a relationship, and all the other complex challenges we've discussed and omitted, it takes one determined individual to get the ball rolling.

This book is dedicated to you and people like you who in each case want to, have to, or are forced to step up to something really big and important, against odds for success. This book is for you, with the hope that your first step will be acknowledging the complexity as you power up to compel the world's latent talent to collectively form the megabrains that pave the way in our era of unrelenting opportunity.

Acknowledgments

WE OWE A DEBT OF THANKS to all of the thought leaders and pioneers in the domains of systems thinking, complexity theory, and management cybernetics. (Especially Stafford Beer, his team of developers and users, and Fredmund Malik, who collectively set us on the course to developing and commercializing our own implementation of the Formula.)

Every one of our customers, especially the early ones and especially the first-time, have taken a "leap" in trusting our Formula in the context of their big challenges. They tried a new approach to strategy, or innovation, or planning, or postmerger integration, or branding, or . . . or . . . or . . . and we thank them. Our stories are your stories, and we look forward to coauthoring new ones with you for years to come.

Thank you to the people at RTI International who first used the Formula in 2014 and loved it so much that they "bought the company."

We are grateful to all the professionals and partners who invested their energy, passion, hearts, brains, and sweat in continuously improving the Formula and delivering top-quality experiences and results. We want to acknowledge those who participated in applying the Formula to an earlier draft of *Cracking Complexity*. In two days, our requisite variety group, including a few of our customers, made this a much better book than it otherwise would have been.

To Bruce, Lindy, and Sarah, thank you for helping us immensely with your thoughts, critique, and contributions, and for keeping us marching toward deadlines.

Finally, to our loving families who have variously offered their own unique contributions over the years: You inspire us. Thank you to Jen, Angie, Rachele, Marisa, Zoe, Jamie, Micaela, and Oakley.

Foreword

OVER THE PAST FORTY YEARS, I've had a unique perspective as an executive coach, working alongside exceptional leaders and their leadership teams. Leaders and teams like predictable outcomes. Most of us like to work in that space where things have been done before. We prefer tried-and-true processes that lead us to known answers.

In the midst of complexity, little is predictable and known answers are scarce. Increasingly, leaders at every level of the organization face complexity; they encounter challenges that seem—on the surface—completely unsolvable with the time and resources they have available.

When leaders confront these seemingly impossible tasks, they often rely on default responses. Some simply adopt an "it can't be done" mindset and refuse to move. Others fight the valiant fight; they boldly apply their most trustworthy tools, processes and partners to the challenge, in the hope that things will somehow turn out well. Both approaches, at their heart, are fundamentally flawed.

That's because—to introduce a concept from David Komlos and David Benjamin—many leaders have been treating complex challenges like they were simply, everyday complicated tasks.

We're used to complicated tasks. We face them every day. Complicated tasks have known, predictable solutions. The required work is often difficult and time-consuming. We may need dedicated teams—or help from external experts—who have specific training and skills, but we can get the job done. We can even estimate the effort required and predict a degree of success.

As you will learn in this book, though, complex challenges are fundamentally different from complicated ones. In a complex challenge, the solution is not known and certainly not predictable. In fact, no single person or small team could, on their own, identify a good—or even a good enough—solution.

For a complex challenge, the degree of difficulty is exponentially higher than with a complicated one. And complex challenges cannot be solved with the tools used to solve complicated tasks. The solution must be created anew.

Senior leadership teams need to make complex, high-stakes decisions all the time: for example, in the context of mergers, strategic reorganizations, and global product launches. These leaders usually recognize the stakes involved, and they sense all the moving parts and interconnections. They may even realize that these situations defy quick and easy solutions. However, leaders often don't detect—or understand—the underlying factors that define these challenges as complex instead of complicated. And they lack a proven way to go about solving complex problems.

The company's success—and often individual careers—ultimately rely on making the right choices in these situations, but leaders usually start by making the wrong choice in how to solve them.

In *Cracking Complexity*, David Komlos and David Benjamin present us with a better way for leaders, at all levels, to find answers to complex challenges and mobilize people quickly, rigorously and reliably.

And that's absolutely pivotal to leadership today and tomorrow. Opportunities have small windows for action. Complex challenges must be addressed quickly, and traditional problem-solving methods that we use for complicated problems simply cannot keep up.

When you have the right people in the room and follow the formula outlined in the book (the same formula that has been used by global companies for years now), you can systematically produce breakthrough solutions every time. Often within just two or three days of work!

If that speed seems difficult to believe, then know that David Komlos and David Benjamin have a two-decade track record with a crème-de-la-crème list of global organizations, mostly at the C-level. They've helped organizations solve incredibly complex problems. This book you're reading isn't a business-school textbook written by theorists. It's a recap of what really happened with real companies solving real problems. This is field research. It has happened. It is happening.

As a leader, I know you've felt the accelerating pressure to solve your organization's most important complex challenges without enough time or resources. Take a deep breath. You've come to the right place. This book serves up the mindset, steps and skills that you and your team will need to crack complexity, so that you can find clarity and build momentum in uncertain times.

It will help you frame smarter questions, uncover opportunities faster, and align your teams more effectively. Along the way, you'll encounter terms such as genetic algorithms, human parallel processing, forced collisions, and requisite variety. These new terms reveal some of the mathematics and data-science that make this approach so effective. And they will help you, as a leader, develop a new way of thinking and problem solving.

Now, many books are great at teaching people how to spot opportunities, but they don't provide you with a process to take advantage of them. That's where David Komlos and David Benjamin shine. Most of this book gives direct answers to help you translate opportunity into action.

Their formula is a step-by-step method to "crack" your biggest challenges. Along the way, you'll find compelling stories and examples. It's got practical nuggets that you (and your team) can apply daily to just be better at routine things: meetings, team-building, collaborating on direction, engaging stakeholders, and so on.

If you're an emerging leader, you will create your reputation on your ability to build teams that can solve complex problems quickly. You will rise through the organization and be presented with increasing challenges.

If you're a senior leader, your legacy will be defined by the high-stakes decisions you make on behalf of the organization.

Throughout my career, I have helped leaders overcome their individual limiting beliefs and behaviors to achieve lasting success for themselves and their teams. I've helped people focus on solving the challenges within themselves so that they can achieve success.

David Komlos and David Benjamin's Complexity Formula provides a powerful approach to external challenges—the ones that require groups to come together. When you get the right minds in the room and structure their interactions properly, complex challenges become solvable. That's the path to breakthrough insights that you and your team can and will implement.

Marshall Goldsmith, #1 *New York Times* bestselling author, *Thinkers 50*—#1 Executive Coach and the only two-time #1 Leadership Thinker in the World

Preface

IN 2001, we were introduced to a motley crew of pure academics and business professionals. They had found each other and stayed connected around one shared interest—the genius of complexity pioneer Stafford Beer and his efforts to turn his insights into something usable. They all wanted to save the world.

We had never heard of Stafford, cybernetics, or some of the obscure geniuses who had inspired him or were his contemporaries, like Ludwig von Bertalanffy, Warren McCulloch, W. Ross Ashby, Norbert Wiener, Buckminster Fuller, Heinz von Foerster, Russell Ackoff, and Fredmund Malik. We met Stafford in the hospital, days before his death. That meeting introduced us to a world we didn't know existed and put us on the path to making some of its bounty mainstream.

Each of us had been involved in various businesses, including jobs at large multinationals, stints with consulting firms, and leadership roles in dotcom-boom start-ups. Now we entered a world of stark-looking, long-bearded scientists whose writings were totally inaccessible to mere mortals, almost written in code, using what seemed to be a secret lexicon. After we understood the true meaning of what we were hearing, we were electrified at the prospect of applying what we learned to a broad range of situations; we realized it could solve for complexity in ways that could produce quantum leaps in performance and growth for organizations and individuals.

Like most start-ups with a *minimum viable product*, we had our fair share of starts and stops, long sales cycles, and existential crises. Road trips, forgettable hotels, poor diets, long visionary conversations, early adopters, huge fans, big detractors. All the while developing and applying an evolving Formula that just flat-out worked.

And then, timing and luck kicked in.

Complexity as an organizational topic had been around forever and had attracted the attention of brilliant academics and others for several decades. Toward the end of this century's first decade, however, business and government leaders became serious about complexity and it entered their collective consciousness.

Fast-forward. When organizations are facing central, confusing, multidimensional challenges and opportunities, they apply the Formula. More specifically:

- When a merger is going south
- When a reorganization has taken place and the company wants to invent its new strategic planning process
- When a company wants to double its business in China
- When they want to take out cost without undermining the consumer experience
- When a business unit needs to be turned around
- When a conglomerate wants to digitize
- When an organization wants to bring a new way of fighting cancer to market

For many years now, we've worked closely with the CEOs of Fortune 500 companies, policy makers, global product leaders, government officials, and the heads of global associations. Each of them has made a deliberate decision to use an unconventional, unfamiliar approach to achieving results faster; they've applied it to their top challenges; the stakes involved have always been high; the first time they've advocated using the approach has always met with resistance; and the outcomes, both immediate and long-term, have been considered unprecedented.

What is also true across each of these situations is that the leaders using our approach know that we are not experts in their business, industry, or sector. Until they experienced the Formula firsthand, they had only a surface-level, abstract understanding of how it works and how it would work for them. They recognized in the moment that the challenge at hand was in a league of its own, that the usual ways of addressing it would likely fail or take far too long, and that they needed to try something different.

Cracking Complexity is about engineering serendipity in the face of complexity. It's about engineering collisions and "controlled explosions" that release massive amounts of directed human energy that had been previously untapped. Humankind has mastered the effective use of controlled explosions in many technical endeavors from automobiles to rockets. These have advanced our societies in leaps forward, all in a very short time. The leaders we've worked with have learned that controlled explosions of brainpower and emotional commitment in large, special-purpose groups, have the same basic outcome: major leaps of progress in compressed time frames.

The Formula we will give you in this book is based on a blend of many scientific and sociological breakthroughs and is itself a well-tested marvel. That means it yields the same outcomes every time the necessary conditions for success are established and maintained for the duration of its application. The outcomes are:

- Full clarity in the face of prior confusion
- Novel, achievable solutions and plans
- Widespread buy-in, alignment, adoption, commitment, and mobilization

All in mere days.

When people collide in the right way, great things happen. And the experience is a deliberate, necessary, and inevitable mix of lows and highs, friction and concordance, divergence and convergence, serious doubt and frustration, before getting to glimmers of hope and eventual satisfaction and, often, elation.

Having brought this to market and scaled it in all manner of organizations, we know the Formula's promise can still smack of fantasy to those who have not applied it, so much so that we can understand the inclination to chalk it up as just that—fantasy and empty promises.

But there's a simple reason why so many top organizations use the Formula: It works on complexity better than anything else out there.

Organizations bring us in recognizing that we're not experts in their industry. They know, however, that we have mastered the Complexity Formula, and it's the outcomes from that Formula they want, and fast.

If you're a CEO or senior leader of any kind of organization, you'll want to read this book, understand the principles it contains, and know that it holds step-by-step instructions on how to tackle everyday complexities and the seemingly intractable challenges that you've been banging your head against for months.

If you're a manager in any function related to, or mired in complex challenges, you'll be able to use this book not just to understand what you're facing but to apply its lessons to solve the problems that bedevil you and capitalize on the opportunities that excite you.

The Complexity Formula is a machine that just works. It has been engineered for our era of unrelenting opportunity and represents the best way to institutionalize the capability to crack complexity. And now we pass it to you, so that you can do so.

CHAPTER **1**

Journey into the Unknown

YOU PROBABLY routinely encounter daunting complexities in your work. It doesn't matter whether you're the CEO of a Fortune 500 company, a not-for-profit executive, a sports team manager, or a feature film studio exec. A slew of head-spinning problems confronts you. You're trying to achieve an ambitious objective and the paths keep shifting in a volatile environment. You're executing a major change program and struggling for sufficient traction. You're attempting to mount a response to a growing number of incredibly agile competitors who always seem one step ahead.

The challenges before you feel overwhelming in the best of times and impossible in the worst.

The good news is that they don't have to be either. Complexity is challenging—in fact, it is *the* challenge—but the challenge can be met, and fast.

We know this because complexity is what we do. We help a wide variety of organizations and systems solve knotty problems. We help people and groups unravel the knots using the Complexity Formula that we'll share with you in this book. The results come with unprecedented speed and traction. Novel answers emerge. Turning points happen. It doesn't matter how confusing, multifaceted, or fast-changing the challenge is.

Any complex problem, creative challenge, or highly ambitious goal can be achieved very quickly, given the right approach.

We'll give you the Formula, step by step, but first we'd like to put complexity in both a historical and philosophical context to help you understand our perspective.

Toffler, Beer, and Hollywood

In 1970, Alvin and Heidi Toffler published the book *Future Shock*, in which they coined the term "future shock" as a personal and societal perception of "too much change in too short a period of time."[1] In that same year, Stafford Beer, an obscure genius in the even-more-obscure field of management cybernetics, gave his inaugural address as the president of the Operational Research Society and said:

> No one can any longer say whether mankind can survive. . . .
>
> Man is a prisoner of his own way of thinking and of his own stereotypes of himself. His machine for thinking—the brain—has been programmed to deal with a vanished world. This old world was characterized by the need to manage things—stone, wood, iron.
>
> The new world is characterized by the need to manage complexity.
>
> Complexity is the very stuff of today's world.[2]

Why are we referencing two thought leaders from the 1970s? Because "too much change" and complexity as "the very stuff of today's world" define our realities now more than ever. And because Stafford Beer is the one who laid out the initial version of the Formula that we've evolved into what you'll read about here.

Many people have heard of *Future Shock*; almost no one has heard of Stafford Beer and his contemporaries. Both Toffler and Beer were warning of complexity at a time that was *exponentially less* complex than today. Organizations and societies faced change, but those were *simpler* complex times. Personal computers didn't exist yet. Millennials wouldn't be born for another few decades. Consumers bought things in local stores.

"Digital" was a term that referred to clocks that were easier to read. Amazon was a river, Apple was fruit, and Google wasn't a word.

Leaps Forward in Large Groups

We're far from being the first ones to recognize that complexity is a huge challenge. Our heritage includes some of the names we mentioned earlier. And over the years, other people and organizations have created a variety of approaches that in isolation and in combination have come to represent the conventional wisdom of how to approach, in part or in whole, complexity. These include in no particular order:

- Agile
- Lean Six Sigma
- Experience centers
- Whole system change
- Scalable learning
- Sprints
- Management consulting
- Design thinking
- Systems thinking
- Change management
- Storytelling
- Online communities
- Crowdsourcing
- Idea management software
- Collaboration software
- Call-an-expert
- Expert councils
- Innovation centers
- Scenario planning

- War-gaming
- Strategic foresight
- Etc.

The inventors and practitioners of these approaches have learned important truths about their subject. For instance: to examine things from 360 degrees; to leverage data; to allow ideas to gain steam before dismissing them; to foster collaboration; to put the user, or the customer, or the stakeholder at the center; and so on.

The Complexity Formula draws from some of these approaches and from complexity science, but what's different is that it's focused on mastering the challenge of *orchestrating large groups of people fast and with whole outcomes*, where others have not. We've focused on engineering how to give large groups the capacity to *sense* exponentially, *absorb* exponentially, and *think* exponentially so that they achieve exponential leaps forward in thought and execution.

Why put the focus there? The answer lies in the red deserts of Santa Fe, New Mexico.

The Santa Fe Institute

The Santa Fe Institute (SFI) began with a series of casual transdisciplinary workshops led by leading academics. The first workshop on complexity was held in the summer of 1986. Operations remained fairly informal until John Reed, the soon-to-be-CEO of Citicorp, reached out to convene a brainstorming session on understanding international finance as a complex system. Reed wanted to understand why Citi's highly capable economists were unable to foresee a major downturn in the Latin American economy. That session led to the creation of a complexity economics program and accelerated the study of complexity sciences at SFI.

Today, the institute hosts a range of projects dedicated to problems in complex systems science, from collective computation to big data and social networks, to thermodynamics and biological systems, and to scaling sustainable cities, all aimed toward the mission of understanding the "shared patterns in complex physical, biological, social, cultural, technological and even possible astrobiological worlds."[3]

As SFI defines it on its website, "complexity" is what "arises in any system in which many agents interact and adapt to one another and their environments." "Agent" simply means individuals or groups that engage in activity. What makes a system complex is not the presence of many agents, but the fact that these agents adapt to and interact with one another in a way that creates unpredictable consequences. Because the behavior of each agent is dependent on another, each agent's action offers opportunities for further interactions, creating complex feedback loops that evade easy analysis. In complex systems, the behaviors of agents cannot be simply "summed" up, for the "whole is more than the sum."

In his introductory book to complexity, John Henry Holland, pioneer of genetic algorithms and University of Michigan professor, provides as an example of a complex system a commodities market where agents buy and sell, adapting their strategies as market conditions change, leading sometimes to "bubbles" or "crashes."[4] For Holland, understanding the interaction of adaptive agents is critical to solving some of the most important problems of the Twenty-first century. These adaptive agents and their interactions are at the core of complexity.

Whether it's SFI or any of the practitioners of the methods and approaches we listed above, untangling complexity in human systems ultimately points to a need to rapidly and efficiently involve, tap into, and force interactions amongst a large cross section of these agents, which in human systems means people. This is the requirement that becomes the biggest (not the only) determinant of success or failure.

The Plight of the Hero

To suggest the magnitude of complexity's impact today, let us draw an analogy to the movies. In the 1970s, Hollywood created many disaster movies about sinking ships, burning buildings, crashing airplanes, exploding zeppelins, plunging elevators, earthquakes, avalanches, floods, nuclear meltdowns, tidal waves, and hurricanes. Each film was about a survival threat to an isolated group of people—each one depicted a single disaster at a time. In most of them, a hero would save the day by making a superhuman effort and rescuing some of the others who survived the initial disaster, and eventually life would return to normal.

The disaster on the screen brought about a complex situation, but each was a one-at-a-time event that could be dealt with and was over by the time the credits rolled.

If today's complexity were depicted in one movie, we'd have simultaneous earthquakes, avalanches, floods, nuclear meltdowns, tidal waves, and hurricanes, each compounding the effect on the others, with all of humankind getting stuck in sinking ships, burning buildings, crashing airplanes, exploding zeppelins, and plunging elevators. Then the aliens would arrive, and a meteor would strike. And it wouldn't end; the disasters would keep coming with accelerating frequency and severity. To get out of this mess, we'd require many heroes, and each would have to become continuously stronger, faster, and smarter to keep up with the mounting disasters. And they'd all have to work together effectively.

We are living in times that are far more complex than even Toffler and Beer could have foreseen. Unfortunately, the vast majority of organizations still approach complexity as if it were the 1970s. They know better—but they still try to deal with problems one at a time and in sequence. They still act as if survival is just a matter of getting off the plane or the elevator or the zeppelin and getting on with business as usual. They still embrace the tenet that you have to "go slow to go fast." The results range from bad to a disaster.

Meet Our Three Heroes

Dealing with complexity these days is like the *hero's journey* trope in storytelling: a hero is shaken from his or her comfortable day-to-day existence, embarks on an adventure, ultimately wins a decisive victory, and then comes home changed or transformed. Except here, the hero is an organizational leader, the adventure is overcoming a complex challenge, and the victory is the achievement of clarity and action that puts the hero and the organization on a new path with the complexity mastered.

We're going to be following the story arc of three heroes who are composites and archetypes constructed from real people and situations we've worked with. We can't use actual names and business cases because those are confidential and central to highly competitive situations and core strategy.

Our three heroes are meant to collectively cover business and non-business situations, challenges, and opportunities, dealing with internal and external dynamics, partnerships, and ecosystems. Each narrative is important for understanding concepts, instructions, and the experience of executing both.

Here are their respective organizations:

1. Plesius Finacorp, a global financial services company trying to get the most from an enormous partnership
2. Doregan, a global consumer packaged goods conglomerate fighting to remain ahead in an increasingly declining industry
3. Micbern, a health system struggling to align and mobilize diverse stakeholders in the state in order to tackle the mental health crisis

We'll be talking about these three individual "heroes," along with others from their respective ecosystems, throughout the book. But first let's eavesdrop on their thoughts.

1. Brenda, SVP of finance at Plesius Finacorp, financial services company

I can remember the day that I realized it.

It was my second year of working here. I spent my first year trying to understand the business of Plesius Finacorp and financial services in general; I came over from a media giant, an entirely different industry. One day, I was reviewing our financial statements and I noticed something that raised a question mark: our partnership with Danley-Ross HealthAge, a network whose members are 50 or older. Danley-Ross provides several benefits to its members, from health insurance to discounts at restaurants to community events in major cities.

On paper, our partnership was fairly insignificant, as it was only bringing in less than 1 percent of our total revenue. It involved us providing discounted financial advisory services to members of Danley-Ross who are retirees or soon-to-be retirees. But the more I asked around to understand the partnership, the more I awoke to its potential. We would get business without having to ask for it, as Danley-Ross would line up its members for us, who would in turn be offered financial planning sessions with our financial advisers at a discounted rate, a valuable perk of membership in the network.

What made me truly pause was, after chasing people with multiple emails and phone calls, I found out that this partnership, despite being in play for just under a decade, had only captured about half a percent of Danley-Ross' network. Given how large their membership is (40 million members), if we bumped that to even 3 percent, that would dramatically increase our total revenue with minimal additional effort or cost on our end. I'm not sure why I seemed to be the first person in Plesius to notice this opportunity, but perhaps because my previous company ran many meaningful partnerships, I was used to examining their value.

Strategic partnerships were led by Trent, who was in charge of our Community Engagement group. His counterpart at Danley-Ross, Sasha, oversaw their Corporate Partnerships function. The three of us came up with a solid list of tactics on how to bump the .5 percent capture to 3 percent over the next few years.

After the meeting, I expected that our respective teams would all hit the ground running. But it was slow going. Leaders on both sides dismissed many of our ideas. A few Danley-Ross people felt that while they do offer corporate discounts to their members as well as educational resources and advocacy, the centerpiece of what they did was community building. Cultivating trust was their number one priority, and they didn't want to spam their community members with a bunch of ads. Plus, our program was just one of many corporate programs they were running, so Danley-Ross felt little urgency.

Sasha simply didn't have enough time to try to convince all the people at Danley-Ross whom we needed to get onboard. Their culture made it complicated and slow to get sign-off and commitment. I was having only a slightly easier time myself within my company, as I was relatively new to Plesius and didn't quite have the influence or relationships to figure out how to convince a lot of people to allocate their time and resources toward this opportunity (nor did Trent, who is quite junior). We are a flatter company, but it's not that much easier to get things done. Everyone was very polite and amenable to my face but never followed through, and it was hard to hold them accountable.

If we don't step in to secure the loyalty of Danley-Ross' members, another financial services or financial technology company easily can. The clock is ticking, and I need to find a quick way to mobilize a whole host of people (20+) from both organizations to align and execute upon a shared strategy—before someone else does so. Everyone knows that more and more boomers are retiring every year, so everyone's angling to find ways to attract and cater to seniors.

There's quite a bit on the line for me too. I want to find a way to resoundingly prove the value I can bring to the table by going above and beyond the traditional responsibilities of an SVP of finance. Identifying this opportunity with Danley-Ross was the easy part—now comes all the hard work.

2. Pablo, CEO of Doregan, a global consumer packaged goods company

I can see the writing on the wall. In fact, I think a lot of people here can. But we're not making any real headway.

When the board brought me on four years ago to run Doregan, I was up-front with them: I've always been impressed by Doregan, it's an enormous company with some of the strongest brands in the industry, but I have my own vision for what Doregan can be.

Consumers have changed. People's preference for clean labels has rapidly moved into personal care and home care products, like soaps and detergents. We are well aware of this, but our products largely are behind the trend.

Yes, our personal care and home care products are still popular, but we need to expand our customer base to include millennials. The retail landscape is also changing simultaneously, which is our even bigger challenge. Channels are proliferating left and right, making it hard for us to maintain consistent pricing and forcing us to spend more to customize SKUs for each channel. People are going online for the everyday goods they need, shopping either at large e-commerce sites like Amazon where we are competing on price, convenience, and reviews, or at vertically integrated, socially conscious start-ups that deliver products to their loyal base with a personal touch.

These days, it's all about "customer insights," but the problem is that we are disconnected from customers because we primarily don't sell directly to them, but to retailers. We know how to manufacture, market, and sell at scale, but we know comparatively very little about customers—and we aren't doing a great job measuring what they are saying about our products on social networks.

We are still mostly focused on our cash cows, which, even though declining, are still making us a lot of money. Moreover, there is simmering distrust and plenty of conflict within our organization between employees who have been here for years and a growing and louder chorus of people who want to change our ways and are frustrated by the slow pace of change. Some of them, especially the millennials, don't get that we're a 40-year-old company with thousands of employees based all over the world. And to make matters worse, our leadership team isn't aligned, so we aren't cascading messaging or pressure consistently.

We have made some changes. Thanks in part to the advice of the consultant we brought on, we've made some smart acquisitions of start-ups. We also tried to revamp some of our classic products, but we got some serious backlash from some retailers and even loyal customers who insisted that our products remain the same. We recently announced a goal to reduce carbon emissions and eliminate plastic packaging, but we are struggling to effectively coordinate suppliers, packaging, logistics providers, and retailers toward the same goals. These hiccups aside, we are still making lots of money. But we're still squarely on the path toward being irrelevant. Bottom line: we need innovation.

You would think with the clarity I have about the clear and present dangers all around us, my fellow leaders would be all about trying new things, investing in new things, figuring out the future core of the business, and so on. But we've been a quarterly-run business forever, and I haven't changed that. We have too many priorities that we're trying to execute when we only have capacity for doing a small fraction of them well, at most. Our team spends too much of our time putting out fires, and we aren't internalizing that the entire platform we're standing on is burning.

3. Alicia, mental health director for Micbern, a health system

I haven't been this busy in years. I've been fielding phone calls, chairing meetings, reading reports, talking to reporters, and attending summits on our state's mental health crisis.

And I feel like I've only really started to wrap my head around how complex this is. It used to be mainly healthcare professionals and mental health advocates who would show up to these summits and conferences. The last summit I went to there were court justices, law enforcement, drug trafficking officers, state commissioners, jail staff—not to mention the usual representatives from public health, hospitals, psychiatry, and disabilities.

The numbers are bad, and they are getting worse. Suicide rates have risen nearly 30 percent since 1999,[5] and serious depression has been worsening in teens, especially girls, for which some say social media is partly to blame.[6] Our largest state prison holds more people with serious mental illness than our largest state psychiatric hospital—and we're not alone: 43 other states also share this problem.[7] Funding for mental health is shrinking, which is *great* timing because Micbern's psychiatric emergency departments are receiving more patients than ever before. There are never enough beds for everyone who needs to be hospitalized, and we are getting sued over how long it takes to get a bed. What's more, we are seeing patients come in not just with mental illness but also serious drug use. All of this is having an impact on our economy; serious mental illness costs America $193.2 billion in lost earnings per year.[8]

To top it off, we are short on workers. We need more psychiatrists, psychiatry nurse practitioners, and physician assistants, especially in our rural counties. I'm kept up at night by the fact that nationally 60 percent of practicing psychiatrists are over the age of 55[9]—what happens when they all retire? My medical school students tell me frankly they aren't going into mental health for a number of reasons—pay disparities, emotional burnout, inadequate staffing, lack of support, and workplace safety.

I spoke to the CEO of our health system the other day about the need, within Micbern, to come up with a holistic strategy for treating our mentally ill patients. He agreed but said that maybe we should turn this into a state-wide strategy. After all, many of our patients come from rural areas of our state or nearby states, as we are one of the few large health systems in the region. The burden of our mental health crisis is far too much for our health system to shoulder by ourselves, and yet somehow it always feels like we are the ones others are looking to for guidance.

I agreed with him, but a part of me felt too tired to even think about it. At the last conference I went to, there was all this talk about "coalition," "collaboration," and "coordination." But my day-to-day job of running and evaluating programs, training doctors, connecting with different divisions, teaching students, managing morale, and engaging in community and patient outreach is more than enough for me.

That said, every day I run into examples of how tackling this crisis will require a system-level effort. Treating a schizophrenic patient, for instance, can sometimes mean coordination amongst police officers, social workers, addiction counselors, and residential treatment centers— not to mention the medical professionals within our health system: the emergency room doctors, psychiatrists, nurses, and so on. Of course, many of my peers blame the closure and defunding of state psychiatric institutions in the 1950s as the reason why people with mental illness have been pushed to the streets, jails, and hospital emergency rooms. Now our state social services, from our jails to our homeless shelters to our hospitals, are operating far beyond capacity. It feels like every move we make ends up creating an unexpected reaction, and we're always scrambling to react and catch up.

There is insufficient consensus on what mental illness is and what it does to a person, what responsibility and agency they have, and little consensus on what successful recovery looks like. We need to get all the right players in the room and aligned on an approach and strategy—I agree. Just spare me from being part of another task force or work group.

What these three heroes need is the capability to make frequent, fast, and effective pauses that successfully set the new and right course while simultaneously mobilizing people for effective, efficient, and sustained execution. They achieved that through the Complexity Formula.

We will interweave each hero's story throughout the book, but not all of them will be featured in every chapter.

The Antagonist

All of our heroes' challenges are akin to changing the tires on a fast-moving truck while the road is shifting underneath. Very difficult indeed. Sometimes, in transformational situations, these challenges are actually far more akin to changing the tires on a fast-moving truck that is barrelling down a road that is no longer a road while trying to figure out what to transform the truck into and executing the transformation—and time is of the essence.

That's complexity.

Now let's return to our disaster film example. Consider the changes today's incumbent movie businesses face. Audiences have changed radically—when, how, where they consume content, and what they want to pay to watch. Distribution is different, as are financial models, merchandising, promotion, and domestic and global markets. On top of this, it still takes the major studios years to put their products out from concept to screen, and that's for the needles in the haystack that make it that far. New competitors in entertainment, however, are putting content onto screens *everywhere* for consumption *anytime* and in many cases much faster. They've been able to start up their businesses with clarity on where things are *now* and where they are heading with better-suited internal processes, culture, talent, capabilities, and partnerships, absent the overhead of the past.

That's complexity too.

Every type of organization needs to find a way to crack complexity, including those in the movie industry, automotive, real estate, health, food and agriculture, retail, manufacturing, oil and gas, governments, and NGOs as well as publishing, gaming, music, and psychology. Complexity also is a growing force in our personal lives, as well as in dealing with societal and planetary concerns.

When you learn to categorize the real challenge in all those domains as complexity, you can discover approaches that apply to them all. That's what this book can give you—mastery of complexity: what it is, what it means to be facing it, and how to find your way in the throes of it.

Let's start to unpack it now.

Categorically Different

Have you ever thought about why humankind has successfully traveled to the moon but companies still have a hard time figuring out how to grow faster than the competition? That we can make interventions using nanotechnology but struggle to turn around the performance of a business unit? That we can provide global access to the internet, but have a really hard time taking a promising product global? And that we can build robots that perform delicate surgical operations, yet we struggle to provide fair and cost-effective healthcare?

We can master highly sophisticated technical and technological challenges because we're quite skilled at making linear connections from one technical feat to the next. But complex, multidimensional challenges are categorically different. They are not *linear*. They are not solved or even solvable through technical prowess. They don't stand still. They don't patiently await solutions. Complexity is a whole different ball game.

The adjective "complex" appeared in the English language in the 1640s; it meant "composed of parts" and had evolved from the Latin *complector* ("surrounding, encompassing").[10] The second half of that word in turn came from *plectere*, which meant "to weave, braid, entwine." A more familiar definition for complexity, "not easily analyzed," is first recorded in 1715.

Think of terms such as "of many parts," "woven together," and "resisting analysis" as they relate to your business. The odds are you thought about or articulated these terms when confronting issues such as how to double the growth of a business, transform a culture, cut costs but not effectiveness, offer a world-beating consumer experience, comply with new legislation, define your innovation agenda, take a product global, respond to the loss of a major patent, merge companies, monetize dormant IP, figure out digital, reinvent the brand, transform your go-to-market, or create a new customer model.

For complex problems such as these, we don't know in advance what's going to work because we are in new territory. Too many factors are at play (known and unknown) that haven't been identified, let alone mastered; rather than linear and observable, the chain of causation is dynamic and obscure. On top of all this, the human factor is different with every complex challenge. People in a given organization may possess silo mentalities, harbor different objectives, and be resistant to change; they may also be ambitious and politically motivated. Thus, a solution that worked in one place at one time won't necessarily work somewhere else or even in the same place at another time, even when the complex challenge seems to be the same on the surface.

That notion doesn't apply to *simple* and *complicated* challenges, two other categories of challenges you routinely encounter, so let's take a moment to understand the differences.

Simple/Complicated vs. Complex

Broadly speaking, challenges are either:

1. Technical in nature, mechanistic, orderly, linear, and completely predictable.

   Simple and *complicated* challenges are technical in nature. Straight-line, step-by-step solutions can be implemented by anyone (simple), or by experts with the necessary expertise (complicated). You solve simple challenges on your own regularly. For complicated challenges, you either solve them on your own if you happen to have the expertise, or, more often than not, you solve the problem by getting experts to do for you what they've done for others many times before.

2. Creative in nature, unscientific, messy, unstable, and unpredictable.

   Complex challenges require innovative responses. These are the confounding head-scratchers with no right answers, only best attempts. There is no straight line to a solution, and you can only know that you've found an effective strategy in retrospect. Your complex challenges are never really solved; you grope your way forward and see how it goes.

Here are some examples to help you differentiate the terms:

- Having a wedding is complicated; having a happy marriage is complex.

- Buying a house is complicated; being a good neighbor is complex.

- Fixing a car is complicated; disrupting the automotive industry is complex.

- Placing a bet on a horse race is simple; placing an informed bet is complicated; the race itself is complex (if it weren't, you'd only place winning bets).

- Completing a paint-by-numbers image of a landscape is simple; painting a landscape on a blank canvas is complex.

- Doing a math assignment is complicated; doing a writing assignment is complex.

- Solving the Rubik's cube is complicated; establishing this product as a worldwide sensation and commercial success was complex.

- Building a rocket that can put a person on the moon is merely complicated; rallying the country to create the conditions where it could happen fast, that was complex.

- Implementing a customer relationship management system is complicated; delivering a winning customer experience consistently is complex.

- Installing a new enterprise-wide accounting system is complicated; taking 10 points out of Selling, General and Administrative (SG&A) without harming the business is complex.

- Rolling out idea management software is complicated; creating and executing on a robust innovation agenda is complex.

- Implementing an Enterprise Resource Planning (ERP) system to enable transformation is complicated; transforming is complex.

Anyone can solve simple challenges by following a checklist. Complicated challenges are best addressed by experts who follow an explicit or implicit checklist and apply "gray hair" expertise. For complex challenges, experts can never guarantee success because a step-by-step solution doesn't exist. Complex challenges are best addressed by the system or ecosystem facing them, possibly augmented by some combination (depending on what the situation requires) of experts, influencers, stakeholders, regulators, system integrators, customers, etc.

Complexity is where only high-variety talent, rapid leaps forward, and trial and error can enable success.

In the complicated domain, knowledge is power; in the complex domain, a fully tapped diversity of talent is power. A linear approach to solving a complicated challenge gets you a solution in time; a linear approach to solving complexity can't keep up.

To paraphrase a famous quote from journalist and scholar H. L. Mencken: "To every complex problem there is a solution that is simple, neat, and wrong."

Renders the Old Playbook Obsolete

Think of a football coach on the field with the league's best playbook, and players who know that playbook inside and out and can execute it on a level that no other players can. Now consider what happens when the coach is told, midgame, that he needs to *transform* the playbook immediately because the entire game is changing, and if they don't change, they will lose. The coach can respond in the following ways:

- Ignore the instruction to change the playbook and continue to execute the existing one.
- Take the instruction seriously, call a time-out, bring the players to the sidelines, and tell them to forget the playbook and figure out a new set of plays, then send them back in and hope for the best.
- Take the instruction seriously, call a time-out, and stand there paralyzed not knowing how to proceed given that each of the choices above will lead to certain failure.

None of these options is viable. If you're our hypothetical coach, you feel like you either have to make a bad decision or no decision at all. Paralysis in this situation is the likely outcome; what has always worked is no longer working, and making a major shift midgame feels impossible.

Complexity does that to you: You knew what you were doing, but what used to work doesn't anymore.

Doesn't Call a Time-out

Much of the wisdom and constructs we were taught come from much earlier times (like 10 years ago, or 100) when things were simpler. Even seemingly unquestionable beliefs and values need to be rethought—the formula for "winning the race" included.

Think of the tortoise and the hare. The story concerns a hare who ridicules a slow-moving tortoise. Tired of the hare's arrogant behavior, the tortoise challenges him to a race. The hare soon leaves the tortoise behind and, confident of winning, takes a nap midway through the race. When the hare awakens, however, he finds that his competitor, crawling slowly but steadily, has arrived before him. The traditional moral of this story is that "slow and steady wins the race." While that may have been true in slower and steadier times, "slow and steady" is a recipe for disaster in today's world, where complexity is a dominant force and exponential curves have replaced linear trajectories in characterizing the pace of change. In the face of your biggest challenges today, you can't be the tortoise because the hare is certainly not lying down to nap anytime soon. To go back to our football coach analogy, the hare doesn't call a time-out.

At the same time, you also can't be the hare. When there's so much to absorb and process, speed alone won't work—no matter how fast you move, you can't outrun hyperfast, quantum-leap change.

Complexity demands a "tortoise-and-hare" hybrid approach that offers a powerful way to deal with a volatile and rapidly evolving set of circumstances. Instead of *going slow to go fast*, tortoise-hare agility means *going fast in going slow to go fast*. Taking a pause to understand what's happening, think it through, decide on the new course of action, and get going again. Changing the playbook while play continues.

Moves at an Exponential Pace

As we've emphasized, simple and complicated challenges are *linear* in nature. By that, we mean step-by-step. Now take a complex challenge like "being a good neighbor." Try something—take a step—like replacing the fence between your yards. What state is your relationship in as a result? What number of possible states could it be in? Did your neighbors agree the fence needed replacing? Did you insist on wrought iron when they just wanted to stay with wood? Did they agree to share the cost of the wrought iron, or did they insist that they should only pay for half of what it would have cost if you had agreed to wood? Now take another step based on the resulting state achieved from the replace-the-fence step. For example, throw a loud backyard party. Now how many states could result? And don't forget to multiply that number of states by the number of possible states after the fence was replaced.

While simple and complicated challenges trace out a straight line in terms of progression from state to state, the number of possible states for complex challenges grows *exponentially*. And they can get out of hand quickly—spiraling up, spiraling down. Don't try to predict the states and chart out the steps. You're dealing with too many: factors; interdependencies between factors and steps; forces at play; unknowns and even more unknown unknowns.

Notice, though, that the demand on the organization *is not* for it to become exponential itself in order to keep up. Rather, it must occasionally be able to temporarily perform exponentially when faced with correspondingly exponential challenges.

Organizational leaders are battling wave after wave of accelerating change, wishing they could match this change with quantum leaps in performance—leaps that their organizations aren't designed to achieve.

Most organizations weren't designed for these times. Their various processes—core business, decision making, financial, innovation, procurement, talent (and so on)—are not agile, distributed, or capable of acceleration when needed; they certainly aren't real-time and continuously running. They are linear in nature and capable of linear pace only.

They have change breaking out on many fronts at once, and just as
they gear up to deal with things like a new ERP, or a customer-centricity
initiative, or big data, or their talent strategy—a new imperative appears,
like China, or cybersecurity, or a new Uber-like entrant into their market.
The traditional large-scale 18-month initiative can't keep pace. But as we
walk through the halls of many large organizations, they've got two or
three or five of them on the go, just as they would have had in the '80s or
'90s when faced with these kinds of challenges.

What's at stake isn't just keeping up with unrelenting and accelerating
change; it's remaining viable and relevant.

Why the Need for a Formula?

Complexity is categorically different.
Complexity renders the old playbook obsolete.
Complexity doesn't call a time-out.
Complexity moves at an exponential pace.

Solving complexity comes down to mastering cocreation in large groups.
Handling complexity as if it is merely complicated doesn't work. Getting better doesn't get you ahead. Getting incrementally faster isn't fast
enough. A bit leaner isn't lean enough. Somewhat more agile isn't agile
enough.

While many conventional approaches and methodologies have positive aspects, they do not deliver the *exponential* capacity that matches
exponential challenges. With complexity inside the organization and all
around it, its multiple facets absorbed by diverse people at different times,
a new, fit-for-purpose approach is required. A new approach that engineers, step-by-step, how to master cocreation in large groups. That's the
raison d'être of the Complexity Formula.

In this book, we'll take you through the details of how and why the
Complexity Formula works. Our three heroes will bring it to life for you
so that you are far better equipped for your own journey into complexity.

We're going to give you a lot to think about and a lot you can use right
away. In terms of the former, we're going to take you through conceptual
building blocks and share metaphors and stories to help you absorb them.

While anonymized and abstracted from customer situations, the stories are all true accounts of various organizations struggling with complexity.

But this would be just another theory book if we didn't also give you instructions and tools. That's the Complexity Formula.

We've tested and refined it continuously since 2001, implementing it in a wide variety of situations and producing startlingly positive outcomes. It is now operating at peak efficiency. It is universally applicable, no matter how complexity manifests itself in your organization.

And beyond your organization, it has big implications for every complex activity, job, pursuit, challenge, sector, industry, and society.

The Journey through This Book

Using the Formula and the stories we'll tell, we're going to take you on a journey that consists of three major destinations:

- The starting point is to separate the complex from the merely complicated.
- The paradigm shift is to go from a scarcity mind-set to an abundance mind-set when it comes to the talent necessary to untangle complexity.
- The breakthrough is the ability to take "power leaps" quickly so that large groups of people can make exponential progress in mere days.

As the next chapters will demonstrate, you have to start at the right place or the entire journey will be for naught. Complex is a lot different from complicated, and by recognizing the differences, you'll be able to view the issues facing you with the right perspective.

The paradigm shift requires you to stop working under the false premise that the solution to complexity resides within a small, scarce pool of talent. Tapping into the abundance of talent available to every organization puts you on the right path to solutions.

Breakthroughs occur when you are able to systematically accelerate the progress that large, high-variety groups of people can make, while also setting them up for effective execution of what they've co-created—with unprecedented speed and effectiveness.

Following this path will yield benefits that are exponential rather than linear. You'll reduce the time line for achieving objectives from months to days. And best of all, you'll possess a capability that works on all manner of complex challenges.

In the coming months and years, these challenges will come at you fast and furiously. Complexity isn't going away. Instead, it's growing and accelerating.

CHAPTER **2**

Getting Started

I T'S NOT LIKE WE'VE NEVER SOLVED complex problems before. We've been dealing with complex challenges from the beginning of time—challenges with no prepackaged solution, that are nondeterministic or seem nondeterministic until a repeatable solution is found.

Humankind's historical search for meaning, through religion, the arts, and a wide range of scientific domains has also been a search for answers to complexities, like how to live a good life, how to lead a community (or nation) to prosperity, how to raise children, and how to ensure survival. In organizations, leaders have faced a variety of complex issues over the years—the need to achieve advantage, maintain relevance, adapt—and everything that entails, big and small.

More recently, the world has recognized, especially from an organizational standpoint, that complexity is as much a discipline as leadership or innovation, and we need to formulate an approach to deal with it. Given all the complex challenges in modern times, and so many trial-and-error attempts to deal with them, we have started to see the patterns, design the models, and formulate sound approaches.

To create an effective approach to meet complex challenges, look back at the wisdom served up by past thinkers and doers. They were all groping for answers to the same overarching question: *"How can we best deal with something we've never dealt with before, without foreknowledge of what's going to work?"* And they discovered and shared a lot of profound insights that contribute to answering that question. Albert Einstein said, "How do I work? I grope." For Sir Isaac Newton, he felt that "no great discovery was ever made without a bold guess."

Now mix in the thoughts and words of those in the past century who have been studying abstractions like systems and complexity, and the pieces start to form an interesting—and surprisingly *singular*—formula that solves for complexity—a step-by-step approach that synthesizes all that thinking into an algorithm that organizations can apply to their complex challenges.

We didn't create the Complexity Formula out of whole cloth. It took centuries of genius thought, wisdom accrued over lifetimes, and much trial and error before the repeating patterns and breakthroughs began to emerge. And, as they say, timing is everything—it took exponential growth in the complexities themselves and in the frequency and interconnectedness of those complexities before people actively started looking for viable approaches. Smartphones are really powerful devices derived from decades of technological advances. What you're about to see is a formula derived from centuries of work. We just pulled that work across the finish line.

Just before we take you through it, it's important that you first understand a few principles that lay the necessary foundation for you to use the Formula.

The Law of Requisite Variety

There is a simply stated cybernetics "law" (in the same sense that Newton's Law is a law) from W. Ross Ashby, the president of the Society for General Systems Research from 1962 to 1964 and a fellow of the Royal College of Psychiatrists. It is known as *Ashby's Law* or the *Law of Requisite Variety*: *"Only variety destroys variety."*

Complex challenges are high variety: Lots of moving parts, lots of dots to connect, lots of factors at play, lots of interconnections and compounding, many facets to be considered and implications to be taken into account. If you're going to deal with all that at once, Ashby's Law says you need to bring a matching amount of variety to the solving process.

- In the kindergarten classroom, there's a variety mismatch: The teacher or teachers don't have enough variety to "destroy" the variety that the children bring into class (in the form of their individual behaviors, maturity, learning styles, knowledge, upbringing, innate skills, health challenges, energy levels, attention spans, and so on). The result is often pandemonium, or at times, 99 percent of the teachers' attention is focused on dealing with the most outlying behaviors in a handful of kids, while the rest get little attention at all.

- Trivia contests are clearly a domain where only variety destroys variety—the higher variety the team, the more likely they will collectively know (or successfully guess at) the answers. Time and again, a table full of complete strangers will outperform a table full of family members or friends who likely have too much in common to carry enough variety for the questions thrown at them.

- The members of an eight-person senior executive team can know a lot about the organization they lead, but can they know enough to set a three-year strategy during times of turbulent change? Do they have enough variety to know what their customers are expecting today and will expect three years from now? Do they know what their employees are really thinking about their jobs, about their workplace, and about their future? Do they have an accurate understanding of what the competition is up to? Are they current on digital, and big data, and cybersecurity as well as lean and emerging markets?

To deal with something complex, you need a high-variety group that can collectively do justice to the complexity.

The Lion on the Desk

The rather extreme example of "the lion on the desk" is one we've been using for years to further underscore the complexity challenge and the meaning of "requisite variety."

Imagine you walk into your place of work one morning, open your office door, and see a lion sitting on *your* desk, licking its chops.

In the blink of an eye, you are able to *sense* the lion, *absorb* the implications of its presence on your desk, *think* about your options, *decide* on a good course of action, and *act* (very likely by turning around, slamming your door, and running in the other direction).

Organizations don't work nearly as fast. In organizations, the sensing, absorbing, thinking, deciding, and acting are all *distributed.* And often, their challenges are not as obvious a threat as a lion in the office. Even when the problems are big and scary, or the opportunities highly compelling, people across and around your organization are seeing them in different ways at different times. Say the challenge is Amazon. They're seeing various versions of Amazon's impact, and they're hearing different things from different customers (some might be competing, and some might be cooperating). The "lion" isn't a single, unambiguous signal in a single place. It's being sensed in various places by varying people.

Are these "sensing" people absorbing the micro- and macroimplications of what they sense? Do they have enough context to fully absorb what's going on, or is it someone else's job to aggregate and triage signals? Say it is. Now you've got sensing and absorbing formally assigned to a small group of "people," with a lot of other sensing going on across many people in distributed (and likely compartmentalized) areas of the organization. You get the picture? They don't!

Figure 2-1   Sensing the Lion

The absorbing of implications and the thinking about what to do about them are also performed by different people. And many of the thinkers are not the decision makers. They're often at least another step away.

And of course, those who decide on a course of action aren't usually the ones who will do the work of executing on the action plan.

Organizations do not have the ability to sense-absorb-think-decide-and-act at the pace of change, whether they are contending with weak or strong signals, shrouded in noise or plain as day. And that lion's not going to wait for you to carefully and judiciously figure it out.

Of note, the lion on your desk is almost certainly on many of your competitors' desks, too. In some shape or form, they are contending with many if not all the same challenges you are. And their ability to sense-absorb-think-decide-and-act is hindered in the same way.

So, while the *elephant-in-the-room* problem is common and well understood, the *lion-on-the-desk* is a first-principle human condition that plagues meaningful progress on all complex challenges. That's a massive opportunity for the ones who figure it out.

Figure 2-2   The Lion in the Office

SATDA and Requisite Variety

When you think about requisite variety, you need to think about all the
lion functions. Who are the . . .

- "Sensors"? Often the front line, and often the people who are left
  out of these kinds of conversations.
- "Absorbers"? Who is taking information from the sensors, compil-
  ing it, organizing it, analyzing, sharing it? IT? Business intelligence?
  Do they have to all be inside your organization?
- "Thinkers"? Corporate strategy? Line management? BU leadership? Executive leadership team (ELT)? Consulting partners? All
  of the above?
- "Deciders"? BU leadership? ELT?
- "Actors"? They could be anyone and everyone: Those who will take
  action in response to the lion on the desk; those who will manage
  the action plan; those who will govern it; and those who need to
  approve it and lead it.

Your requisite variety needs to take SATDA, all five lion functions, into
account.

The 'Data, Information, Knowledge, Wisdom' Model

The DIKW model has its origins in the field of information science as
early as 1955 or 1974 (depending on whom you cite as the originating
thinker). It is known as DIKW because it most commonly encompasses
data, information, knowledge, and wisdom, but like any good model it
has evolved to include other components over time, and it has various
representations (e.g., as a pyramid or hierarchy in some other form).

It appears in a more refined form in Russell Ackoff's 1999 book, *Re-
creating the Corporation: A Design of Organizations for the 21st Century*,
where he refers to it in adage form:

An ounce of information is worth a pound of data.
An ounce of knowledge is worth a pound of information.
An ounce of understanding is worth a pound of knowledge.
And an ounce of wisdom is worth a pound of understanding.[1]

Data, information, and knowledge are important raw materials, but in their typically fragmented abundance, they don't easily lead to understanding and wisdom; rather, they hamper that progression and thus become another facet of the complexity.

What should act as stimulus for fast and smart decision making instead muddies it.

As writer, consultant, and teacher Clay Shirky says, "Abundance breaks more things than scarcity."[2] With data, information, and knowledge being abundant, the advantage that people, companies, and societies enjoyed because they possessed proprietary knowledge assets is now diminished or completely gone, and what remains both scarce and coveted is understanding, wisdom, and speed of execution. And so, the leadership imperative now is to equip organizations to leverage data, information, and knowledge, from anywhere and everywhere, into building those higher levels of proprietary understanding and wisdom.

And as we'll continue to explain, requisite variety, properly harnessed and unleashed, is what cuts through the noise to bring about understanding and wisdom.

Shared Understanding

Shared understanding is the key to transitioning organizations from linear data/information/knowledge toward wisdom and execution. The pursuit of shared understanding, done well and done fast with all the right people involved, yields startling insights. It serves as the foundation for incredible creativity and the ability to align on and mobilize around what's got to be done. It's what makes complexity manageable.

Shared understanding is what you've achieved when the right people have separated out and agreed on the pertinent signals. While noise can drown out the organizational ability to think and move, shared understanding is where clarity lives. After sensing, absorbing, and thinking as a group, shared understanding means you're poised for astute decisions with a critical mass of buy-in and mobilization for action.

The Myth of Talent Scarcity

The Law of Requisite Variety and the idea of the lion on the desk should disabuse you of the notion that the talent required to solve your big challenges is scarce. It's not. It's all around you.

At times, on certain challenges, frustrated leaders tell us that they feel the team they've assembled around them and the partners they've brought in for help aren't getting the job done. Nobody's good enough to deal with what's going on "out there," nothing they do works or works fast enough, and everybody's complaining about being too busy and feeling overwhelmed.

It's like baseball managers wishing for a whole team of five-tool players who can hit for average, hit for power, steal a base, throw the ball a mile, and cover the whole field with their speed. But, even if you have a handful of these five-tool players, they are also the people who delight customers, deliver excellent products and services, get the most out of others, and so on. As a result, they are buried deep in their day-to-day activity, and far too valuable to pull from it.

So, there is seemingly a dearth of talent.

That's what we call the myth of talent scarcity. But why a myth? Because these leaders are not suffering from a scarcity; they are suffering from the inability to tap into, combine, and benefit from the abundant talent that exists within and around their organization, and to effectively augment it with the skills, knowledge, experience, and expertise that they can only find outside.

When it comes to dealing with complexity in the context of strategy, growth, and innovation, the bulk of the talent needed isn't scarce, it's just locked away (like the shale oil that used to be locked away until the technology came along to extract it in an economically worthwhile way).

Yes, key people are busy. Yes, most people struggle to think outside their day-to-day roles and outside the proverbial box, and yes, others have broader exposure to what's going on "out there." But that doesn't mean that the answer is to wholly outsource the sensing, absorbing, thinking to someone else (for example, a traditional consulting partner). You can do better than that.

Key people can make the time, if the time needed is short. Individuals don't need to be capable of solving these enormous challenges on their own, but networked together efficiently and effectively. Given access to others who have the data, information, and knowledge they lack, they are each very capable contributors.

It's all about scaling the right talent—largely from inside the organization and, crucially, also from around the organization and its ecosystem, quickly, efficiently, and collaboratively. In this way, they can figure out the right few things to do, then return to work prepared to do them and to help others do them.

Dealing with Perceived Scarcity the Old Way

The prevailing outsourced approach to strategy, growth, and innovation is the traditional management consulting model, a model that applies the following logic: *"The scarcity of talent and capacity in industry means you need to outsource the research and the thinking to us. We'll do the heavy lifting. You'll also greatly benefit from our feet on the ground because— again—your organization needs the additional capacity and brainpower our people represent. AND because our people are scarce top talent, they cost a lot of money."*

The traditional management consultancies have thrived because:

- They do have the time/capacity most of their client organizations lack;
- They are liberated from all the perceived and real constraints their customers' people experience;
- They have specific expertise their customers need;
- They have a lot of brainpower;
- They are good at navigating silos.

The flaw, though, is believing that the best way to benefit from these attributes is to opt in to an interview-based, hub-and-spoke model: *The answers are "out there" and all we have to do is to hire a partner to bring them to us.*

That model is not suited to complexity.

- It taps into the important contributions of requisite variety through a linear sequence of interviews (linear, even if scheduling of interviews allows for some to happen in parallel). This isn't fast enough, and it doesn't build connections among the people who collectively hold the answers.

- It filters all the rich variety represented by those people through the small group of people at the hub and leaves the thinking and creation of a novel solution to that same small group.

- It doesn't directly connect the people who hold the answers, it doesn't break down the walls between them, and it doesn't engage them or mobilize them for execution.

The right way to benefit from outside experts is to combine them within the requisite variety group. The right way to find answers is through conversations, not interviews. The right way to prepare people for execution is to engage them in cocreating their way forward, not to have someone else tell them what they have to do.

S-Curve Leaps

In laying out our perspectives and definitions surrounding complexity in Chapter 1, we said that the key to solving complex challenges ultimately comes down to mastering cocreation in large groups. And because of the (seemingly) exponential pace of change related to complexity, the demand is to match that with an exponential capacity to take leaps.

The natural state of human beings and organizations is linear—proceeding through the day-to-day with linear action: One step at a time, following carefully thought-out, proven processes and procedures that reliably get you from Point A to Point B. When an exponential change threatens, that linear pace doesn't cut it. The requirement is to leap forward in a way that adjusts the course accordingly. After making the leap, it's fine to settle back in and continue acting linearly but on a new path that is in line with the change.

It looks like this:

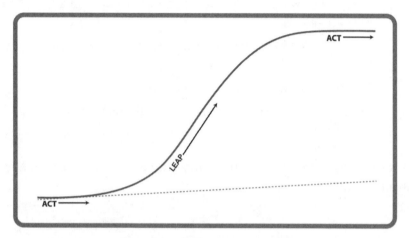

Figure 2-3   Act Leap Curve

ACT-LEAP-ACT will be an important mnemonic for the Complexity Formula—and we'll show that in the next chapter, but for now, what does "a leap forward to adjust course" look like?

- It's a manufacturing company that figures out in days what to do about a pricing/margin threat being created by Amazon.
- It's a drug company rapidly developing the commercial game plan to seize the dominant position in new ways to combat cancer.
- It's a chip company dealing with the decline of PCs and the rise of smartphones and tablets.
- It's a payments company dealing with chip technology.
- And it's a company that makes chips (the food kind) figuring out how to meet emerging consumer preferences.

These are all real examples where the Complexity Formula was used to take that leap.

In the *lion on the desk* analogy, we said that individuals can sense-absorb-think-decide-act in the blink of an eye, but systems can't. The Complexity Formula is all about getting all the right people (requisite variety) together in one place together to:

- Share and absorb the signals that they have individually and collectively sensed;
- Jointly think about how all those pieces fit and what the implications are;
- Decide what course of action is required;
- Co-create a shared plan of attack that will guide their actions going forward.

By executing all the steps in the Complexity Formula, you get an effect that looks like this:

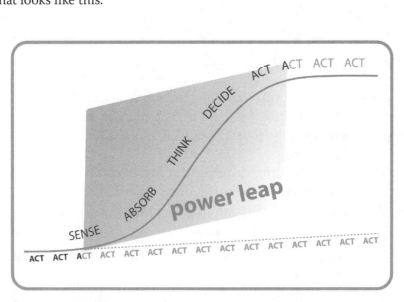

Figure 2-4   Power Leap 1

It's the people who span the lion functions who will take the leap. And they will be fueled by the data, information, and knowledge they carry in and learn from each other, accelerating through the noise together so they arrive rapidly at shared understanding and ultimately wisdom and creative judgment—so they can decide on the right course of action and execute accordingly.

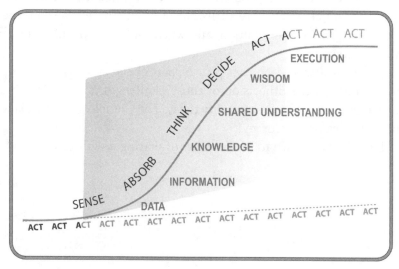

Figure 2-5   Power Leap SATDA

The Language of a New Paradigm

Requisite variety, the lion on the desk, SATDA, DIKW, talent abundance, and S-curve leaps are increasingly the language of organizations that are consistently successful in solving for complexity.

To pull it all together:

- The *requisite variety* of people who match the variety of perplexing challenges and seemingly unattainable opportunities
- Can and must work together to collectively *sense, absorb, think, decide,* and *act* in order to ascend from *data, information,* and *knowledge* to *shared understanding, wisdom,* and *execution*

- At a pace that matches the pace of those challenges and opportunities, *leaping* from current course and speed to a new course and speed without missing a beat.

The talent to do so, the people who will drive these leaps, isn't scarce; they're abundant, and they're all around you. They're relatively inexpensive, they're part of the solution, and when mobilized in the right way, they're extremely fast.

The capability to leap past your biggest challenges and to seize the opportunity on the other side of those challenges is the single most important organizational capability today. The Complexity Formula will unlock this capability for you.

Let's now get down to the business of sharing it with you.

CHAPTER **3**

A Picture Worth 418 Words

WITH THE RIGHT APPROACH, solving for complexity can be incredibly fast and change can be incredibly fast—in contrast to what we've all been conditioned to expect.

The Complexity Formula tells you how to go about tackling complexity yourself and with the help of people in your internal and external networks.

We'll introduce you to its overall flow here. Then, we'll show you how to apply it, step-by-step.

All the steps in the Formula are complementary and build one upon another (looping in some places) to deliver rapid leaps, accelerated SATDA, rapid wisdom, clarity, and traction in the face of complexity. Each of the steps also offers stand-alone insights, an "aha!" here and there, and takeaways that can be applied in isolation from the rest of the other steps.

Here is the bird's-eye view:

- Steps 1–5 are about setting things up;
- Steps 6–9 are where you and a requisite variety group of people spend a few days figuring things out; and
- Step 10 is what follows the completion of steps 1–9, when a mix of immediate wins, short-term tactics, and longer-term initiatives have emerged.

The Complexity Formula: Solving for Complexity in 10 Simple Steps

1. **Acknowledge** the complexity.
2. **Construct** a really, really good question.
3. **Target** a requisite variety of solvers.
4. **Localize** the solvers.
5. **Eliminate** the noise.
6. **Agree** on the right agenda.
7. **Put** people on a collision course.
8. **Advance** iteratively and emergently.
9. **Change** how people interact.
10. **Translate** clarity and insights into action.

You may have noticed that the mnemonic we mentioned earlier, "ACT LEAP ACT," is spelled out by the first letter in each step.

Note that in the illustration that follows, there are actually two loops in the Formula: An inner loop driven by the iteration in step 8—depicted by the gray triangle with the three-loop at its center; and an outer loop that sends you back to step 1 as you must acknowledge new complexities that are revealed to you by the Formula and apply it again on those challenges.

Solving a complex challenge requires iteration (the inner loop) to power people through accelerated parallel processing and cocreation. It also may require repeated application of the Formula (the outer loop) to drill into new complexities (as you realize, for example, that growth will require a new talent strategy and big data) or to repeat the Formula on the same challenge but in other geographies, business units, or brands, for example.

There's a lot going on here. The next 10 chapters will explain it all.

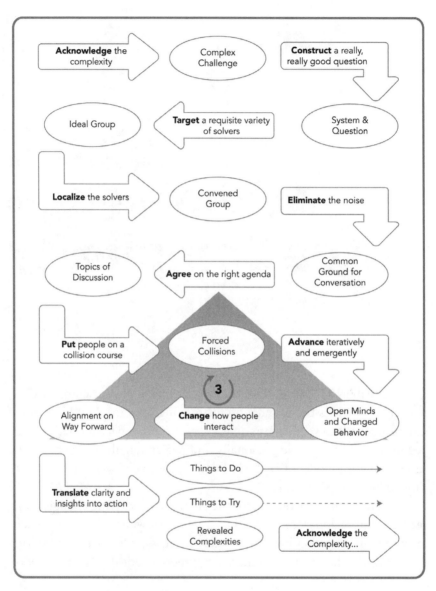

Figure 3-1   10-Step Highlight

CHAPTER **4**

Step 1.
Acknowledge
the Complexity

RECOGNIZING THAT YOU'RE NOT IN CONTROL of your complex challenge provides the foundation for moving forward. Yes, we know it can be difficult to step back as an established, proven leader with a track record of guiding people personally and professionally and say, "I don't know. I'm confounded. I'm stuck. I don't have the answers. I'm not sure how to look for the answers."

When it comes to looking for the answers and driving change, many leaders operate under the prevailing wisdom that when things get particularly confounding, they can always outsource the challenge to a consulting firm. But what happens when the consultants can't deal with the situation

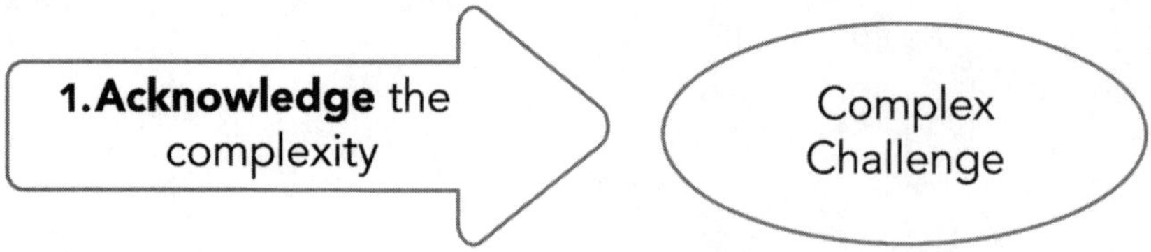

```
┌─────────────────────────┐
│ 1. Acknowledge the       ───▶        ⬭ Complex
│    complexity                          Challenge
└─────────────────────────┘
```

Figure 4-1   Step 1

any better than you can? *Now* you're really forced to admit defeat: "I am not up to solving this challenge."

What's interesting is that it's not hard to admit defeat in the face of a *complicated* challenge, like, "I don't know how to fix my car, so I'll hire a mechanic." Or "I don't know how to install accounting software, so I'll hire a software integrator." Or "I don't know how to set up my iPhone, so I'll bring it to the Apple store." When it comes to "technical" challenges, we seek expert help all the time.

As a leader, people around you expect answers, guidance, strategy, clarity, confidence, decisiveness, and . . . *leadership.* They want you to establish objectives and map a way forward. But you're staring at the situation and don't know what to do.

Acknowledge the complexity. Don't pretend that this is like the simple or complicated problems you faced in the past. Don't hope that a way forward will emerge from the mist. Shift your own paradigm from "I know the solution" to "I know what I don't know." Accept it and go after it.

Would Blockbuster's story have ended differently? What about Kodak? Or Sears? Did they acknowledge the complexity? If they did, did they approach it appropriately and quickly enough?

Acknowledging that change is coming fast, that the same model that brought you to a dominant position is quickly becoming obsolete, that your leadership team is resting on its laurels, that customers (or voters, or photographers, or shoppers) are angry or merely dissatisfied and have new choices, that a new technology is opening the door to unexpected competition . . . that all of the above demands a well-thought-out response *yesterday.* The first step is acknowledging that, recognizing that there are no known answers, that no outsourced provider is going to figure it out for you—at least fast enough—and that the old way of figuring things out isn't going to work anymore.

Acknowledge the complexity.

And think of the opportunity. Think of the release your organization will feel when you get traction again. Think of the power of a leap forward instead of more months of inaction. Think of your competition stuck in the same place and watching your organization surging ahead. Don't passively accept the complexity. Embrace it and *decide* that you need a leap, then prepare to engineer one.

Acknowledge the complexity *and* the opportunity.

How Do You Know?

Determining whether a challenge is complex is as easy as asking these questions:

Have you solved the problem before and then been able to implement that same solution successfully in a variety of similar situations?

If you said "yes," then it's complicated.
If you said "no," then it's complex.

Additional Questions to Ask	Answer	Complex?	Example
Would a thorough description of the challenge be exactly the same as it was previously?	Yes	Likely not	Installation of accounting software
If the circumstances were different last time, does that matter?	Not really	No	Implementation of an ERP system
Would the experts who solved it charge a fixed rate to do it again?	No—they would have to account for unknowns that significantly affect time and effort.	Likely	Postmerger integration

Is the solution closer to science than art? Is it cause-and-effect?

Yes—it's complicated.

No—complex.

Additional Questions to Ask	Answer	Complex?	Example
Is there a reliable and predictable interaction of component parts?	Yes, cause-and-effect	No	Car engine
Could a user manual be written on how to solve it?	Yes	No	Bookcase assembly
Is there a creative component?	Yes	Yes	Movie script
Would two "experts" bring about the same result?	No	Yes	Talent strategy
Can success be assessed unambiguously?	Yes	No	Science experiment

Is there a checklist someone could use to solve it? Could there be?

Yes—it's complicated.
No—complex.

Additional Questions to Ask	Answer	Complex?	Example
Is there a known sequence of steps to follow to solve it?	Yes	No	Testing software
Once it is solved, could you write instructions on how to do it again?	Yes	No	Rubik's cube

Is there an in-house or outside expert available who has solved it before?

Yes—it's complicated.
No—complex.

Additional Questions to Ask	Answer	Complex?	Example
Would they do it again for a fixed price?	No	Likely	A consultant on change management
Would everyone agree it was solved the first time?	Yes	No	A plumbing repair

Additional Questions to Ask	Answer	Complex?	Example
Could the expert teach you or some other expert to do it?	Yes	No	Printing two-sided copies
Has the expert solved it many times before, or just the once?	Many times	No	Developing a website
Is there a chance the expert was lucky the first time?	No	No	A pilot flying a plane

Is there a packaged solution you could buy?

Yes—it's complicated.
No—complex.

Additional Questions to Ask	Answer	Complex?	Example
Is it shrink-wrapped with a picture of the solved challenge on the cover?	Yes	No	A model airplane
Does the packaged solution automatically work wherever it is deployed?	No	Maybe	Setting up a document management system

Additional Questions to Ask	Answer	Complex?	Example
Is the problem solved as soon as you "open the box" and follow the instructions it contains?	Yes	No	Buying a new PC

Are there only a few "unknowns"? Are there only a few "unknown unknowns"?

Yes—it's likely complicated.

If there are many "unknowns" and "unknown unknowns"—likely complex.

Additional Questions to Ask	Answer	Complex?	Example
Can the unknowns be easily known? And once known, is there a section of the instructions you can then follow?	Yes—if I go get some more information, it's a step-by-step process from there.	Likely not	Set up of a new television, instructions for many cable configurations
Can you think of any reasonable risks that might prevent you from solving this?	Yes	Likely	Changing the company's org structure

Additional Questions to Ask	Answer	Complex?	Example
Is there a human dynamic that could reasonably derail the solution?	Yes—there are people who might resist, throw up roadblocks, or actively sabotage the solution.	Likely	Implementing account management

When the answers point to complexity, start by acknowledging that. That's step 1.

Case Study: Pablo, CEO of Doregan

A note: We will interweave each hero's story throughout the book, but not all of them will be featured in every chapter. For this chapter, we'll focus on Pablo's story.

Pablo is the CEO of Doregan, a multinational consumer product goods company. It is a large, 40-year-old company that is struggling to be relevant amidst changing consumer preferences and buying habits.

A few years into my time as CEO, I held a series of town halls to unveil what I thought should be Doregan's new-and-improved manifesto and a revamped business strategy for the next five years. There was a lot of hype leading up to this unveiling. I had hired a top-notch consultant who worked with us for almost a year on creating this manifesto and strategy. I liked their work, but not everyone on my executive team (half of whom are nearing retirement) fully bought in.

"I'm worried we are so obsessed with chasing what's new that we are neglecting our long-standing products and brands," someone on the team said.

I understood the feedback, but I pushed ahead because I was certain that this was where we needed to go as a company. During the town halls, I outlined how we would compete in a global economy where norms about the environment, health, brands, and shopping were rapidly changing on a planet where extreme climate events are increasingly disrupting product supply. I announced that we were going to embrace "lean" operations, become much more environmentally friendly and more transparent in our products and packaging, increase our investment in e-commerce especially when it comes to capturing and analyzing customer data, and make it easy for consumers to enjoy our offerings. I made it clear that we were venturing into new territory, as we'd traditionally relied on tried-and-true solutions, and that we were going to need bolder, newer ideas.

The town hall spooked a lot of the old guard within Doregan, people who have worked in our company for a long time and were loyal to our brand and how "we've always done things." There was an explicit tension between them and the newer vanguard of employees, most of whom were millennials, had different work habits and weren't held back by as many sacred cows. I received a flood of feedback after each town hall, ranging from "I miss the old Doregan," to "Why do we feel insecure about who we are compared to flash-in-the-pan start-ups?" to "My friends can't believe me when I tell them how we do things here; we're so behind and outdated."

I could deal with the outright conflict and simmering anger—but what was more frustrating than anything else was that most people went back to whatever it was they were doing before. Yes, there were pockets of change, mostly among people who were already believers. But the message wasn't resonating throughout the entire workforce, not in the way we needed for us to transform our business. And the PowerPoints that our consultant gave us were left sitting on our hard drives, downloaded but rarely opened.

Don't get me wrong, their proposed strategy was full of smart industry insights; we wouldn't be where we are without their expertise. But there were so many unique, moving parts to our challenge—workforce tensions, product problems, brand questions—that we needed a solution that really fit who we are. And while the consultant did interview a diverse cross section of people to produce their smart recommendations, many of our employees were still dragging their feet. They didn't feel like they were a part of the solutions we came up with, and top-down pressure was clearly only going to go so far. Redirecting our company was going to require a lot of people across different regions, functions, and levels to align on the gravity and magnitude of the problem and then create and truly buy into a shared strategy.

I had a complex challenge on my hands.

CHAPTER 5

Step 2. Construct a Really, Really Good Question

AFTER ACKNOWLEDGING THE COMPLEXITY, where do you go from there? A great "quote" attributed to Albert Einstein—we put "quote" in quotes since there's some debate if he actually said it—may provide direction: "If I had an hour to solve a problem and my life depended on it, I would use the first 55 minutes determining the proper question to ask."

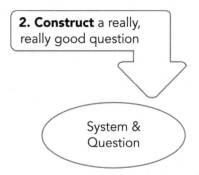

Figure 5-1   Step 2

What is the right question to ask? Let's examine the rationale behind this foundational step.

Defining the Challenge in the Form of a Question

Once you've categorized the challenge as complex, what you would normally do to deal with simple or complicated challenges isn't going to work.

For a complicated (or simple) challenge, all you have to do is name it, using a fairly straightforward label like: "Install the new accounting software," "Plan my wedding," or "Fix my car," and from there, bring in an expert who will ask the necessary questions to configure a known solution. For "Plan my wedding" the questions might be:

- When is it?
- Do you want an indoor or outdoor setting?
- What sort of ceremony are you looking for?
- How many guests?
- What kind of food?
- How much do you want to spend?
- (Etc.)

These and other questions are on the expert's checklist, and the answers lead to step-by-step actions to be taken.

With a complex challenge, however, while you could think of a straightforward label (like "Double the business," "Outpace the market," or "Take the brand to the next level"), this drives deeper questions about the challenge itself, which results in a better expression of the challenge, not a solution. That's exactly what you need to get going: a better expression of the challenge. Which brings us to our First Rule of Q:

First Rule of Q

Use questions about the complicated to **solve** the challenge. Use questions about the complex to **define** the challenge.

Before you can find clarity, you have to start with clarity on the question to ask. We spend time up front working with organizational leaders just to arrive at a good expression of the challenge in the form of a single, big question. When it comes to their challenges, we ask them to think about:

- What's at stake? What happens if you don't address this?
- What's the opportunity? What can you achieve once you've successfully tackled this?
- What's the system facing this challenge? Who will act? Who will feel the impact, good or bad? Who needs to inform this?
- Who will own the resulting plan? Your entire enterprise? A business unit? A product team? A department? Your ecosystem?
- How long do you have? What's the window for action? And what's the window for outcomes?
- Is there a tangible goal or set of goals?

Only after answering these questions can we get to a really good question that does justice to the challenge.

What constitutes a really good question? A question that is as clear and as concise as possible, while being detailed and open enough so that it:

- Engages all the right people and catalyzes great conversations.
- Gives boundaries to the challenge without biasing or unnecessarily constraining the answers.
- Calls for action, names who will act, and conveys a sense of urgency for action and results.
- Sets an aspirational, stretch goal that is within reach, but only if things change.

Getting the question right gives you and other leaders a handle on the challenge; it gives your people clarity on what the organization needs to solve for; and it gives you the essential starting point.

Where to Jump In

Because of the entanglement of factors that make up the complexity, you might be wondering how to ask about the whole thing, or whether it is enough to ask a question that gets at only a few of the more obvious aspects of the challenge. For example, should you ask: "How do we become the market leader?" or: "How do we fend off the threat of that new competitor in our market?" (which is but one aspect of the question about how to become the market leader).

When the challenge is central to the organization, any first step is going to be a doorway into the entire challenge. If you start by talking about customer experience, for example, the conversation will drive to solutions for that subject *and* inevitably uncover issues and work to be done on adjacent and connected themes (like technology enablement, business process, operational risk, etc.). That's the Second Rule of Q:

> ### Second Rule of Q
> When it comes to jumping into complexity, do that from any part of the deck because it's all one pool.

Making It Interesting

The last bit we'll give you here is about the phrasing of the question, the goal it contains, and how compelling it is.

- The question might get under people's skin, and often that's okay because complexity isn't comfortable.
- There's a fine line between aspirational and beyond-the-realm-of-possibility, and each will have a distinctly different impact on the people being given the question: The former revs their engines; the latter can flood their engines until they come to a sputtering halt.

A good gut check on the question is how people react to it. Are they uncomfortable with it because it challenges the status quo, sets the bar high, or suggests a lot of work needs to be done? Conversely, are they completely comfortable with it because it's easy to answer? Don't necessarily retreat from what you think is a good question because people are reacting negatively, and don't be satisfied if people aren't pushing back.

Make sure it's interesting and will spark the necessary conversations.

Third Rule of Q

If the question is an irritant, leave it. If the question is a salve, change it.

Why Do Questions Go Wrong?

There are three main reasons questions go wrong:

Fear of How People Will React

Whoever is crafting the question doesn't want to anger anyone, offend, or scare the teams that have worked so hard on this challenge for the past two years. These are all legitimate concerns *and* they also present opportunities to wake people up, give them a sense of urgency, agitate them, make them reflect on and learn from past mistakes, and challenge them to do better.

It's important to reassure people, thank them for their efforts so far, and make them more comfortable with their place in the world—*after* you've shown them the difficult question. The complexity won't get resolved if it's not confronted head-on. This fear is what leads to safe questions and in-the-box answers.

Fear of Looking Bad

The person or team formulating the question might be worried about how it makes them look to be asking it. Are we showing weakness to our people? Will they think we're not doing our job?

Having acknowledged the complexity, the question needs to reflect what's been acknowledged. It may not feel great to admit to it in the question, but that's the reality.

Faulty Assumptions that Introduce Bias

In drafting a question, faulty assumptions can derail the best intentions. In some cases, for example, we've seen leaders assume that the organization's vision, strategy, values, and key messaging are well understood by the organization, when they simply aren't. This means that what they thought was the right question given where everybody *should be* is precisely the wrong question because their people aren't where they thought.

How to Construct a Really, Really Good Question

Complexity is not easily articulated. But trying to address a challenge you haven't named is like trying to complete a crossword puzzle without the grid.

The output from this step is that really, really good question. And as Einstein would suggest, it's worth spending some time on.

Compel, Rally, Catalyze

The question should compel people to talk. It should connect with their passion. It should be relevant, important, interesting, resonant, and at least a little bewildering to them. The question should not oversimplify, ignore, or unduly glorify the past. It should be hard. The tension or friction being created by the complexity should be reflected in the question.

Here are some blasts from the past that resulted in power leaps (we've taken the liberty of emphasizing the phrases that made these questions stand out):

Question	What Stands Out
What must we do now and over the next 12–18 months so that we **grow earnings by 300 percent** over the next 4 years while **maintaining acceptable margins** (20 percent or better) and **continuing to be a great company to work with and for**?	The built-in tension of growing earnings and margin without making the organization a miserable place to work
What must we do now and over the next two years to **capitalize on existing or emerging opportunities** in our external environment, in order to ensure sustained long-term growth?	The open-endedness of "existing or emerging" opportunities
What must we be **doing differently** over the next 12 months and beyond to increase our patient funnel and the speed at which we are able to find, diagnose, and get patients on the path to getting better?	The subtlety of the phrase "doing differently" versus "doing
What must we do to evolve our customer-facing capabilities over the next 2 years to achieve **genuine insight and understanding into customer drivers and barriers**, build the necessary skills to **change our behavior** accordingly, and leverage these skills to **outperform the competition**?	The implication that we don't currently have "genuine" insights and understanding about our customers and that our skills and behaviors aren't what they need to be to compete

Question	What Stands Out
What do we need to **adopt, let go of, or keep** to create an environment that fosters a growth mind-set within our Contact Center, and **what is all the work that we need to get done** over the next 6 months as a result?	"What is *all* the work that needs to get done" recognizes that there's lots of it, better than the same phrase without the word "all."
What changes to the entire customer experience do we need to make to **turn every customer into an advocate** for us?	EVERY customer advocating for us? That certainly raises the bar.
In the next 12 months, what must we do to drive necessary changes in **mind-set, action, and behavior** to **fully realize** the benefits of operational risk management across the enterprise?	Takes a very dry legal-financial-risk conversation to the very human realm of hearts, minds, and behaviors
What is the **best** strategy to pursue with the objective of becoming the **world's leading** innovation center in 10 years?	Not just the strategy, but the best strategy. Not just a great innovation center, but the world leader.
What must we do to develop and leverage data and analytics across the enterprise as a differentiator and as a means of **fulfilling our mission** and **overachieving** on our strategic priorities?	Takes "big data" out of the technology realm and into mission and strategic priorities
What can we do now and over the next 2 years to get **greater value with more efficient expenditure** on our IT projects?	A good way to say "more with less"

Question	What Stands Out
What must we do now and over the next 18 months to firmly establish talent development as a capability that gives us **a competitive advantage**?	Talent not just for talent's sake, but for a competitive advantage

Bound the Challenge

When our customers are facing challenges that affect every aspect of their organization and overall vision/mission/strategy, they usually ask us where to point the Formula: "Do we talk about all facets, or pick something smaller in scope to start on?" "Do we talk about the entire organization, or pick a business unit to start with?" "Do we go after all of the complexities, or pick one to deal with first, like blockchain?" And so on.

Here is what we probe for:

- Where are the stakes the highest?
- Do they have convening power to bring requisite variety together?
- Is there an 80–20 factor with respect to how to carve up the scope, so that if significant progress is made within this one business unit (for example) or on the "Uber challenge," it will have a disproportionate impact on the overall result being sought?
- What will come next? Is there an enterprise-wide group that is ready to lead and manage and communicate about the resulting action plan, or are we more likely to get strong follow-through in one specific area of the business or another?

Based on these and other factors, you can choose a narrow or broad scope. Ultimately, when bounding the challenge, remember the Second Rule of Q: "When it comes to jumping into complexity, do that from any part of the deck because it's all one pool." Pick somewhere to start based on the above factors, and you'll inevitably get to everything that matters.

If you now look back through some of the questions we just showed you, you'll see that many of them set a clear boundary around the challenge, and some set no boundaries beyond targets to be achieved. Here are a few again with commentary on what the boundaries are or are not:

Question	Bounding without Bias or Constraint
How do we succeed (despite ourselves and all else that stands in our way) at evolving to a fully functioning account-based business?	We know what go-to-market we're evolving to—the rest is up for discussion.
What must we do now and over the next 12–18 months so that we grow earnings by 300 percent over the next 4 years while maintaining acceptable margins (20 percent or better) and continuing to be a great company to work with and for?	We have to grow earnings, maintain margins, and continue to be a good place to work. How and where we do that is to be discussed.
What must we be doing differently over the next 12 months and beyond to increase our patient funnel and the speed at which we are able to find, diagnose, and get patients on the path to getting better?	This is about finding, diagnosing, and getting patients to treatment, not the treatment itself.
In the next 12 months, what must we do to drive necessary changes in mind-set, action, and behavior to fully realize the benefits of operational risk management across the enterprise?	This is just about operational risk management strategy.

Question	Bounding without Bias or Constraint
What must we do to develop and leverage data and analytics across the enterprise as a differentiator and as a means of fulfilling our mission and overachieving on our strategic priorities?	Data and analytics as a differentiator and a driver of mission and strategy; nothing else
What must we do now and over the next 18 months to firmly establish talent development as a capability that gives us a competitive advantage?	The focus is solely on talent development.

In general, notice that if there's any bias baked into these questions it's around time frame, objectives and, in a few cases, decisions already made that are offered as "givens." None of these questions presupposes answers or introduces opinion that isn't meant to be there, as modified versions of the questions above might:

- What is the best strategy to pursue with the objective of becoming the world's leading innovation center in 10 years *in a new, internationally accessible, technology-supercharged building*?

- What *inexpensive* changes to the *frustratingly poor* customer experience (*especially call center*) do we need to make to turn every customer into an advocate for us?

Obviously, we're kidding with these examples, but in fact it's hard to separate premeditated bias from accidental bias—they look the same. Either of the above examples could be a good question if the additional bias is there for good reason. The more important takeaway is to actively look for any bias you're packing into the question and consider why it's there. If you can't rationalize it, remove it.

When it comes to time-bounding the question, there are actually two time periods at play: one is the timing for the call to action; the other is the timing associated with the goal statement. An example of the former is "What must we do now and over the next two years"; an example of the latter is "to hit $5 billion in sales annually by 2023."

Some actions will have to start immediately on "Monday morning." Some actions will start and finish within the planning window expressed in the question ("over the next two years"). And some actions need to start during that period but will carry on longer.

Call for Action and Name the Actors

Identify the system facing the challenge. Is it a department, a brand, a function, a region, the whole organization, the organization plus some of its partners, or an ecosystem that includes your organization? It's easy to get this wrong or not to consider it at all.

Name the system. And if you can't, think about that. That means people are probably going to be ambiguous about the issue when they ponder the question. Consider these examples:

Organization	Questions about the System
Pharmaceutical company about to introduce a new cancer-fighting drug	Is the system your oncology brand team, or is it the network made up of all practitioners who participate in the treatment of the tumor types relevant to your brand?
Product company launching a new product	Is it the company, or does it also include the entire value chain that is responsible for getting that product into the market and the hands of end users?

Organization	Questions about the System
City working on its gridlock problem	Is it the city? Is it the city plus all of the transportation authorities and companies that service it? Is it everyone who travels into and out of the city every day?

This clarity will help you identify who the "we" is in the question when you ask what "we" must do, and it will clarify who needs to be convened as you get to later steps in the Formula.

Set an Aspirational Goal

Without belaboring this point, look back at the earlier questions we showed you. You may not always recognize the goals embedded in those questions as aspirational, but that's only because you don't know the organizations asking those questions.

In every case, the question wasn't easy to answer because the embedded goal or goals would not have come about at current course and speed. The goals reflected a new trajectory for the organization, and that's part of what made the question engaging.

Stretch goals force people to think beyond the same-old-same-old solutions and encourage bigger and bolder ideas. In some cases, stretch stretch goals lead to really big ideas. The danger is giving stretch stretch goals without the freedom to explore what it would take to achieve them. To ask a group to come up with two times incremental growth (above current plan) while telling them not to add any budget or resources—that's just a turnoff. If there are real constraints that can't be removed, make sure the stretch goal is within reach with creative thinking.

Every Word Matters

Even subtle wording changes can have a substantial impact on your question. For example, start with *"What must XYZ Inc. do to adapt to the disruptive forces in our market?"*

Version of Question	Commentary
What must XYZ Inc. do to adapt to the disruptive forces in our market?	When? What forces?
What must **we** do to adapt to the disruptive forces in our market?	This just went from XYZ Inc. acting on its own to a joint effort between and amongst all those convened.
What must we do **now and over the next year** to adapt to the disruptive forces in the market?	A planning window! We're looking for 1-year tactics!
What must we do **starting now and over the next year** to adapt to the disruptive forces in the market?	This just got more interesting . . . things don't necessarily need to start and finish in the next year.
What must we do starting now and over the next year to adapt to **Amazon's impact on our market**?	No need to figure out and align on what the disruptive forces might be . . . it's all Amazon. *(Note that this could be a mistake if there's more disruption beyond Amazon.)*
What must we do starting now and over the next year to adapt to the disruptive forces in the market **so that we remain the market leader for the next 3 years and beyond**?	A planning window, and now an outcomes window and a goal. That changes things.
What must we do starting now and over the next year to adapt to the disruptive forces in the market so that we **become the market leader and double growth each year over the next 3 years**?	A stretch goal. Wow, that's going to require some real change and out-of-the-box thinking.

Version of Question	Commentary
What must we do starting now and over the next year to adapt to the disruptive forces in the market so that we become the market leader and double growth each year over the next 3 years **without affecting our current margins**?	Wait a minute. A bunch of things we could have talked about doing just got shut down. Warning! Warning!
What must we do starting now and over the next year to **fight off** the disruptive forces in the market **by introducing innovative and differentiated products**?	Why are you asking me if you already have the answer?

You get the idea. A lot is riding on the careful phrasing of the question.

A Question-Building Exercise

Let's build a question together.

Question with Placeholders	Consider Replacing the Placeholder with. . .
What must . . .	Must—to signal urgency and no turning back Can or should—to signal you're asking for ideas Will—to grant authority to the group to decide
. . . we do . . .	We—the people in the room We all—calling for individual and group commitment

Question with Placeholders	Consider Replacing the Placeholder with...
	XYZ Inc.—the company is looking for its plan and probably including outside advisers in the discussion.
. . . now . . .	Now or starting now—calling for immediate actions
. . . and over the next 3 years . . .	Over the next 3 years—about as long term as people can think
	Year and beyond—looking primarily at the short term
	Over the next few years—more open-ended about time lines
	Over the next year—looking for short-term tactics
. . . and beyond . . .	Opening up the planning window for future ideas
	Allowing for things that start in the time frame but may not finish by then
. . . to double the business . . .	Insert your own aspirational goal here.
. . . without affecting margins . . .	Insert your own constraint here to add a balancing tension, whether financial, work-life-balance-related, customer-related, or all of the above and a few other things.
. . . while continuing to be a great place to work . . .	
. . . while significantly improving the customer experience . . .	

A note: Here and in the following chapters, we will narrate our heroes' stories and share our perspective on what took place.

Pablo

Pablo is the CEO of Doregan, a multinational consumer product goods company. It is a large, 40-year-old company that is struggling to be relevant amidst changing consumer preferences and buying habits.

A question that resonates

When we first started working with Pablo and a few members of his team to craft the question, there were conflicting opinions. Some wanted to ensure that Doregan wasn't forgetting its legacy products and trusted in the history and longevity of their brands, while others wanted Doregan to innovate in its products, branding, and supply chain. What emerged was a question that tried to do everything:

> Given the changing market and consumer preferences, what must we do now and over the next 12 months and beyond to transform, so that we fully capitalize on new categories and products, position our established products for maximum profitability, and ensure we thrive well into the future?

They received frank feedback from a few more people that it wasn't the right question because it wasn't solving the real problem: Why are our products losing relevance? They ultimately agreed on the following rephrasing:

> What must we do now and over the next six to 18 months across the enterprise to make our products relevant again and drive double-digit growth while maintaining acceptable margins?

They really wanted to get the question right, and in so doing had to invite others to contribute and even challenge them. Pablo knew that for the strategy to work this time around, he had to engage many more and different types of people and secure their commitment.

Brenda

Brenda is SVP of finance at Plesius Finacorp, a financial services company, which has a 10-year-old partnership with Danley-Ross HealthAge, a seniors association. The partnership has been vastly underperforming compared to its potential.

A question that sets the bar too low

Brenda was working on drafting the best question that would help the two organizations—Plesius and Danley-Ross—maximize their partnership. So she enlisted a core group of eight people from both organizations who were directly or indirectly involved with the partnership to create it. After some discussion, they came up with:

> How can Danley-Ross HealthAge and Plesius Finacorp improve the
> current partnership to double the number of users over the next
> three years?

Because of the hierarchical structure of Danley-Ross and the polite, friendly culture of Plesius, the question had to be vetted by more than 20 people. The word "change" had been taken out of an earlier draft and replaced with the word "improve," and a fairly comfortable target (200 percent over the next three years) had been negotiated, amongst other tweaks to the question. The question had gone through too many edits to appease too many people.

After the question was confirmed, Brenda confided in us that she felt the number was too low and the time frame too long (she thought four times growth was actually feasible fast) and didn't believe it would get people thinking outside of the decades-old box they were in.

This partnership, after all, had been going for almost 10 years. People were used to doing things the way they've always done them; only Brenda, the new person to the conversation, felt any urgency to shake things up and seize the opportunity.

We advised her that if she wanted bolder ideas with bigger payoffs, she should think about shortening the time line to two years and raising the target. We'd seen how "safe questions" play out before: The group settles into a fairly comfortable exercise of figuring out how to tweak the machine *just enough* to deliver the number that was within reach. There will be agitators, big-thinkers, and outsiders in the group, but others often filter out their ideas because they are beyond the scope of the question (in terms of hitting the number). The group arrives at a set of incremental, play-it-safe solutions with the "bold ideas" shelved for future discussion.

Brenda nodded when we told her this but said there was only so much she could do. She did manage to alter the question in the end:

> *What can Danley-Ross and Plesius Finacorp do to change the trajectory of our current partnership and grow users by 500 percent in the next two years?*

Alicia

Alicia is mental health director at Micbern, a large health system in the southwest with a network of healthcare facilities and affiliated universities. It is working to mobilize organizations and institutions throughout the state to tackle the mental health crisis.

A question that reflects what's really going on

When Alicia worked with the CEO of Micbern to draft the question, they came up with this:

> *How can healthcare organizations in our state work together in new ways to improve outcomes for patients struggling with mental health issues?*

They wanted the question to be ambitious—to encompass the whole state—while specifically focused on treatment. After they sent the question around to a group of people, they received lots of comments. Some of the hospital's doctors commented, "Everyone keeps complaining about lack of beds, but half of our psychiatric beds these days are taken up by pretrial jail detainees who are ordered there by the court. There is only so much we as healthcare professionals can do." A few social workers employed by the hospital said, "Part of our job is to ensure that patients have a supportive place to go back to after being discharged, but we can't do that when there are so few residential treatment facilities available because of a lack of Medicaid funding for that type of care."

A few psychiatric nurses wrote back to comment, "Taking care of patients requires taking care of the workforce. We feel like the psychiatric department is last on Micbern's priority list. But it's larger than that—we need to address the fundamental disparities in government reimbursements, insurance policies, and salaries in mental health versus primary care." And some patient advocates wrote in to say, "We're sick and tired of being treated like we're 'crazy' and 'violent' and don't know what's best for us. We have to address the stigma and stereotypes of mental illness. And by the way, we're people, not patients."

It became clear that the scope of the question was too prescriptive and too narrow to reflect all the dynamics and factors that fed into the mental health crisis. The question that Alicia and her CEO had to answer was: If we expand the scope to include nonhealthcare representatives, do we think we can still bring the right people into the room to answer the question? They deliberated and decided that they were going to aim big.

Their new question was:

What do we (all of us in the room) need to do individually and together in order to drastically turn the tide of our state's mental health crisis in the next two years?

CHAPTER **6**

Step 3. Target a Requisite Variety of Solvers

A FTER YOU'VE ACKNOWLEDGED the complexity and created the right question, recall Ashby's Law of Requisite Variety: "Only variety destroys variety." It's time to apply this law to identify your solvers.

Step 3 is about identifying the requisite variety of people to match and absorb the complexity. Your goal is to include the necessary perspectives, characteristics, roles, functions, hierarchical levels, and so on. That's a lot to account for, and the easiest thing in the world is not to account for it. But if you shortchange *requisite* variety, you're setting yourself up for no or partial solution and weak execution.

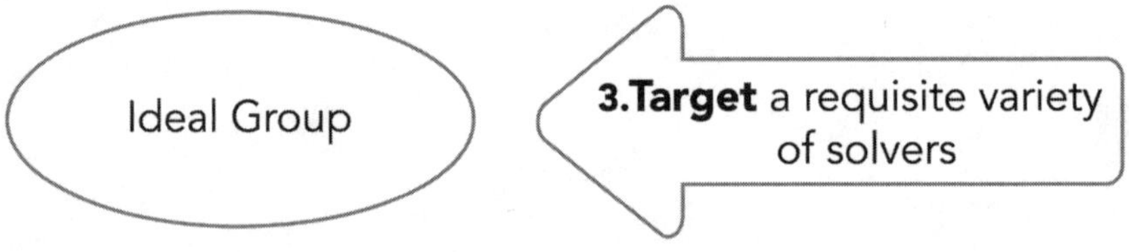

```
                                        _____
 _____                      / 3.Target a requisite variety
(                  )          <        |    of solvers
(   Ideal Group    )          <        |
(                  )          <        _____
 _____                       
```

Figure 6-1   Step 3

70

After many years applying the Law of Requisite Variety to a wide range of systems and the challenges they face, we've created the following structure to enable rigorous examination of variety:

- **12 zones** that define an individual's role, place in the system, knowledge and expertise, and perspectives on the past and on the future
- **13 characteristics** of people, spanning human dimensions including basic demographics, thinking style, personality, attitude, and influence

Not every situation requires coverage of every zone or every characteristic. The framework allows for comprehensive thinking about what does apply on a case-by-case basis.

Doing Justice to Variety

As you consider variety, it's important to take a broad view of the organization, including:

- The system(s) it participates in
- The partners it works with
- The environment it delivers value to and receives value from
- The challenge being faced
- Parallel or analogous organizations and systems with similar challenges that they are facing now or have faced in the past (if applicable)

The 12 zones of variety will guide you through that thinking so you're covering:

- Those from inside your operation—the sensors, absorbers, thinkers, deciders, and actors; the visionaries; the historians; and the front-liners;

- Your inner-circle partners, or confidants, as well as the rest of the allies in the market with you;

- Market experts, futurists, reality shapers, and envoys from your market, your environment, and other environments;

- The vanguard, out in front already dealing with the complex challenge, and veterans from previous, similar challenges;

- And the response team that will be assembled and mobilized to execute on the action plan to address this challenge.

The 13 characteristic cross-checks, in contrast, will help you identify the rest of the attributes you need to cover in the list of people you include in your group. Not where they're from, but who they are. The softer stuff:

- Personality, thinking style, strength on a team;

- Basic demographics;

- Attitudinal factors;

- Stake in the challenge;

- Other hats they wear;

- Influence and authority as they relate to the challenge.

With practice, the 12 zones and 13 characteristics will become a natural way to think about who will be able to contribute unique perspectives in a meeting, who can act as a resource for an existing team, and—certainly—who is a critical contributor to requisite variety on a given challenge.

The trick is keeping your eye on "requisite." The variety word alone can easily lead you to hundreds or thousands of people. Getting the variety with a minimal number of people is where the fun lies—and what makes the Complexity Formula work best. When it comes to the "requisite" word, it's all about efficiency in your selections.

The 12 zones, the 13 characteristics, and the variety matrix that we'll introduce shortly are tools to help you do justice to variety. We'll jump into greater detail about how to use these tools to choose requisite variety on the next few pages. Feel free to skip the details if they're not useful to you right now.

How to Choose Requisite Variety

In the diagram of the 12 zones (Figure 6-2), you'll see each identified numerically, overlying an abstracted landscape.

Starting from left to right, demarcation points separate the system from its market, from the surrounding environment (which we prefer to call the "reality" of the system and its market), and from parallel realities where there are potentially valuable comparisons to be made and lessons to be learned (for example, other industries facing analogous challenges, or other geographies, or other product lines).

Starting from bottom to top, you'll see the past, present, and future. At the top is a looming complex challenge, which we've positioned in the "future" in the sense that it's ahead, not behind. The black arrow that has its origin in the present but points to the future represents the response to the challenge. It starts in the present because there may already be efforts

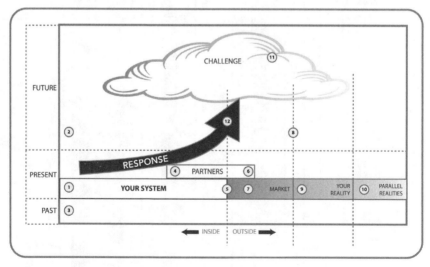

Figure 6-2   Challenge Cloud

12 Zones of Variety

Zone	Could Include...
The System	
1. Operation	Hierarchical, functional, geographical, product, BU cross-section
2. Visionaries	Board, senior leadership, strategists
3. Historians	Long-tenured
4. Confidants	Partner organizations who know you well
The Market	
5. Front-Liners	Sales, account managers, marketing, market intel, business intel
6. Allies	Partner organizations in the market with you
7. Market Experts	Customer organizations, competitors, consultants
8. Futurists	Researchers on the market
The Extended Environment	
9. Reality Shapers	Politicians, regulators, media, public
10. Envoys	Other comparable industries, geographies, products ...
The Challenge	
11. Vanguard and Veterans	Experts on the challenge, veterans of similar challenges
The Response	
12. Response Team	Doers, executive steering committee, PM, communications

Figure 6-3   12 Zones of Variety

underway, but it swings its attention to the future because the response is intended to bring about a new state for the system and its market.

In Figure 6-3, you'll see each of the 12 zones and a label for the talent you're looking for from each zone. As you're reading through it, keep it in the context of whatever challenge you're facing. The "Could Include . . . " column is not calling for you to be exhaustive, but rather selective. Remember we're looking for "requisite" variety, not full variety. The question is "What's the minimum representation required?" not "Who are all the people who possibly fit that description?"

And to bring you back to the lion functions from earlier, here's where you're most likely to find the sensors, absorbers, thinkers, deciders, and actors.

The list of 13 characteristics we showed you earlier are important considerations as well in choosing the people to include in requisite variety. The zones identify people more or less based on their jobs; the 13 characteristic cross-checks give you a handle on the intangibles in that mix of people. If you're choosing among the executive leadership team, who's most open to change and willing to be challenged? If you're choosing from the IT department, who's the biggest skeptic? Among your agency partners, which person always seems to listen first and come with great insights later?

We'll get even deeper into the how-to in a moment, but for now think about all the important differences to bring into the search for answers—strength lies in engaging those differences, in the form of requisite variety.

- The 12 zones and 13 characteristics give you a rigorous frame for the variety you're looking for.

- The lion functions / SATDA should help you think about who to include from each of the inside-the-system zones.

- Your org chart will also offer you a backdrop for thinking about variety (as long as you keep in mind the scope of the challenge/ question and don't get lured into the politics of inviting everyone so as not to offend anyone).

- And then, ask yourself, Is this the best I can do? Have I minimized redundancy, while covering as much variety as possible? What are the dynamics this group, together, will create?

13 Characteristic Cross-Checks

Characteristic	Could Include...
Person	
Personality Type	E.g., Myers-Briggs profile
Thinking Style	E.g., Synthesists, idealists, pragmatist thinkers, analyst thinkers, realist thinkers
Team Strength	E.g., Belbin team roles
Demographics	Age, gender, cultural background, etc.
Attitude	
Toward Challenge	Believer, cynic, neutral
Toward System	Passionately positive, optimistic, worn down, pessimistic, active naysayer
Toward Change	Guardian of status quo, willing to change, change advocate, active disrupter
Personal Stake	Potential loser, potential winner, or unaffected
Other Hats	
Other Specialties	Vertical (e.g., industry) or horizontal (e.g., change management, innovation, blockchain, etc.)
Past Jobs	Other functions, other products, other BUs, other companies, ex-customer...
Influence	
Authority	Decision maker, budget approver, leader
Internal Influence	Credible voice / actor inside the system
External Influence	Credible voice / actor in the market and/or the environment

Figure 6-4 Characteristic Cross-Checks

Lion Functions

Zone	Most Likely Lion Functions
1. Operation	(Internal Complexity) Sensors, absorbers, and thinkers
	(External Complexity) Absorbers, thinkers, deciders, and actors
2. Visionaries	Thinkers, and deciders
3. Historians	(Internal Complexity) Sensors
4. Confidants	(Internal Complexity) Sensors, absorbers, and thinkers
5. Front-Liners	(External Complexity) Sensors, absorbers, and thinkers
6. Allies	(External Complexity) Sensors, absorbers, and thinkers
11. Vanguard and Veterans	(External Complexity) Sensors
12. Response Team	Actors

Figure 6-5   Lion Functions

The Variety Matrix

It's time to enter the variety matrix.

The rows and columns in the variety matrix are the 12 zones and the 13 characteristics, respectively. The first task, therefore, in building your own version is to translate the zones and characteristics to your situation. Warning: you may end up with 40 rows and 30 columns, so use a spreadsheet.

Those are tasks A and B in the picture below.

Tasks A and B—Fleshing Out Rows and Columns

As you dig into the operation, for example, your fleshed-out list might include representation from:

- Four different business units
- Five different geographies
- Marketing, IT, HR, training, finance, legal, and other head-office functions
- Etc.

Once you've fleshed out the list of visionaries, it might include:

- Senior leadership team
- Office of corporate strategy
- The board
- Etc.

And so on, down the list of zones.

As for the characteristics represented by the columns, if you use Myers-Briggs for personality types, you might choose four specific personalities (of the 16), you could list five specific demographics you want to make sure to cover, and so on across the columns.

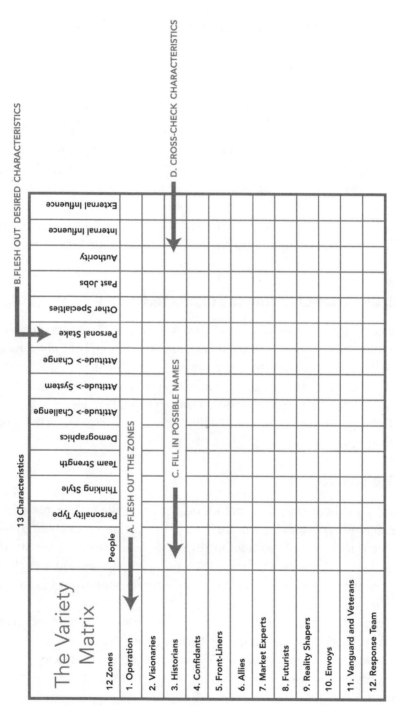

Figure 6-6 Variety Matrix

Now, for the fun part: it's time to start filling in names.

Task C—Naming Names

Here, the job is to arrive at candidates who collectively cover the desired zones.

To do this, build the list of names somewhere else and put a check mark next to each row when you've satisfied it. Some people may fit multiple rows (e.g., someone who represents both a BU and a geography you're trying to cover), so list them once and put a check mark next to each row they cover.

When you're done, transfer the one or more names that cover each row to the People column. You'll likely see some redundancy that you can eliminate later.

Task D—Cross-Checking the Characteristics

Now going back to your raw list of names from task C, see which characteristics they cover. For all the names in the People cell of a given row, check the characteristics that are covered.

If you uncover any key gaps in the characteristics you're seeking, add the necessary names and put them in the appropriate row(s).

Once you've hit all the zones and all the characteristics, you've got your long list.

Refine and Repeat

Now it's all about squeezing names off the list while maintaining full coverage. Where you've got more than one name next to a given zone, can you remove people without losing coverage of the characteristics? If you lose a characteristic unique to one person, can you switch a name somewhere else (e.g., choose a different person from IT) to fill the gap?

Keep refining and repeating until you're convinced you've got great coverage. That's your ideal requisite variety group.

As you were eliminating people from your original list, keep those names handy because you may have to return to them to replace those who aren't available.

Further Guidance

Increasing Your Odds

Later, when you get around to inviting people to join you for a few days to help untangle your challenge, you'll inevitably get some no's. The variety matrix will help you track the impact.

Your long list of candidates will also be important during this phase to remind you of who else you were considering and what they cover.

To increase your odds of achieving requisite variety (especially when you're targeting outside experts), choose the key people on your list and do everything you can to secure their calendars and commitment (including choosing dates that work for them, instead of dates that are best for you). Commitments of influencers create a domino effect. Once invitees get it—they see that other experts will be there, that this is a special event, that they are part of a hand-picked group—they become much more receptive to attending.

Having run the Formula with requisite variety groups for years, we know how critical inclusion of external voices is to untangling your complexity, leaping to a new trajectory, and getting the most from your own ecosystem. Requisite variety includes those who see and know things you and your people would never have thought of or encountered. This means reaching beyond your organizational borders for people who may lack your internal savvy about the company but possess different perspectives and expertise. They may ask the dumb questions that turn out to be profoundly important. For instance, an organization is embarking on a strategy of digital transformation, and the internal members of the group are focused on cost, speed, and usability issues. A professor who has written a futuristic book on the implications of digital on society is invited to be part of the discussion, and she asks this question: "How will digitizing many tasks and responsibilities affect what you describe as your 'humanistic' culture?"

Using Proxies

Below you'll see an expanded version of the 12 zones containing some additional guidance.

12 Zones Expanded

Zone	Could include...	Internal Proxy	% of Variety
The System (40%)			
1. Operation	Hierarchical, functional, geographic, product, BU cross section		35%
2. Visionaries	Board, senior leadership, strategists		
3. Historians	Long-tenured		5%
4. Confidants	Partner organizations who know you well		
The Market (30%)			
5. Front-liners	Sales, account managers, marketing, market intel, business intel		20%
6. Allies	Partner organizations in the market with you	Channels, vendor relations	
7. Market Experts	Customer organizations, competitors, consultants	Customer advocates, call center	10%
8. Futurists	Researchers on the market	Market research	
The Extended Environment (10%)			
9. Reality Shapers	Politicians, regulators, media, public	Regulatory, public affairs	5%
10. Envoys	Other comparable industries, geographies, products	Market research	5%
The Challenge (10%)			
11. Vanguard and Veterans	Experts on the challenge, veterans of similar challenges	Research, office of innovation	10%
The Response (10%)			
12. Response Team	Doers, executive steering committee, PM, communications		10%

Figure 6-7 12 Zones Expanded

The rightmost two columns are reflective of two common questions we get:

- What if I can't bring my customer into the conversation? (Or something similar, where you can replace "customer" with any external 'market experts'). The proxy column suggests that internal customer advocates or someone from the call center can join the group specifically to represent the customer point of view.

- What should be the relative representation from all of these zones?

An internal proxy for an external stakeholder can successfully contribute to requisite variety if they are the right person to do so and if they are instructed that they've been invited in to represent the external voice. The viability of this method comes down to the people selected and how in touch they actually are with the voice they represent.

Ensuring Balance across Zones

As for the relative representation percentages, obviously that comes with a "more or less" qualifier, but more importantly, you're looking at averages that aren't at all hard and fast because different challenges will mean different ratios.

A challenge related to a complexity heavily impacting customers, or playing out amongst customers, likely requires a stronger market voice in the room. A more inwardly oriented challenge (like making our company more attractive to the millennial workforce) may require stronger representation from internal functions (like HR and IT) and a larger cross section of the business units, and less from the market. (Although you can also see how the market, in this case the market for potential millennial hires, may require a strong voice.)

A Few Examples of NonObvious Participants

By now you've understood the depth and breadth of thinking that goes into identifying requisite variety. But to put a fine point on some of the nonobvious inclusions, consider these examples:

- An application of the Formula that convened a cross section of health stakeholders for a conversation about "America's health" included a disruption expert from high tech;

- A car company included a customer experience expert from the entertainment industry in their conversations about the dealership experience;

- A call center asked an ex-employee to come back and share her experiences (both before and after she had left the organization) in an initiative around the consumer experience;

- A national cancer alliance included the leader of another national service, so he could share his knowledge about how to make things happen nationally;

- A pharma company doing postmerger integration included a participant from an oil and gas company who had recently gone through a successful merger and acquisition with similar scope, scale, and intent.

Common Mistakes

When you're determining who should be included in your complexity challenge, it's easy to make well-intentioned mistakes, such as:

- Targeting all the usual suspects—the in-house strategists, the subject matter experts, the outside consulting group. We're not saying don't invite them. We're suggesting that you won't have requisite variety if these are the only people in attendance.

- Inviting based on political pressure. People who have little to contribute to the discussion end up detracting from it.

- Allowing invitees to decline and appoint their own delegates. Keep your runners-up list around and fill in gaps from that list. Handpicking participants enables you to find people who bring at least one (and sometimes several) of the variety components you seek (e.g., the millennial who is analytical, new to the organization, just fresh from a position with a key competitor).

Here's a more complete list of common mistakes when selecting requisite variety:

Mistake	Risk	Mitigation
Being political about your invitations	You get of a bunch of the same perspectives instead of requisite variety.	Exclude people and blame the numbers. Explain to them how they'll be involved before and/or after.
Excluding the customer from a discussion about the customer	This will always get mentioned and affect your credibility.	If you really can't invite customers, invite proxies who work directly with them and tell them they're there to bring in the customer voice. Survey customers ahead of time.
Too little external voice	Nobody challenges the status quo; nobody thinks out of the box; you don't know what you don't know.	Think in terms of 10–20 percent external. Find good external points of view and beg them to "bring it."
Too much of one constituency	A function or managerial level or team dominates, preventing other voices/ideas from being heard.	Actively pay attention to just-enough coverage. Better to uninvite some people if you have to.
Leaving out the senior execs	They see and know things others don't—in other words, they are part of requisite variety.	They will often try to beg out because they don't want to suppress or dominate. Invite one or two senior execs—the ones who will get it right.

Mistake	Risk	Mitigation
Avoiding the cynics	You give them the right to object later; you can't deal with the valid reasons for their cynicism or anticipate those things in your planning.	Bring them in. Embrace them. Actively seek them out. They will become your strongest advocates when you involve them in the right way.
Inviting the wrong external partners	What you think is requisite variety isn't because the external voice is not being honest, more worried about protecting a contract than telling you what you need to hear.	Choose who to involve carefully. Tell them you're expecting them to challenge you and that your partnership is on the line if they don't.
Not serving youth	Things are moving so fast, the youth are the only ones keeping up— meaning you make recommendations about things that already exist without knowing they exist. Not to mention the absence of youthful energy and fresh perspectives.	Youth must be served! Include them as a key demographic to cover. There are often "rising star" lists that you can tap into to find the best and brightest.

Mistake	Risk	Mitigation
Agreeing to involve people who can't commit to being there	Removing themselves for part or much of the time means the zones and characteristics they were supposed to cover aren't covered. You also lose the powerful connections they would have made with others.	Get a commitment to full and dedicated participation. If they aren't willing or able to give you that, thank them and move to a good substitute on your list.

Brenda

Brenda is SVP of finance at Plesius Finacorp, a financial services company, which has a 10-year-old partnership with Danley-Ross HealthAge, a seniors association. The partnership has been vastly underperforming compared to its potential.

"What about Holmes?"

We were in a meeting with Brenda, Sasha (the head of the partnership in Danley-Ross) and Trent (the head of the partnership in Plesius) to discuss whom to invite for a two-day gathering to answer this question: *What can Danley-Ross HealthAge and Plesius Finacorp do to change the trajectory of our current partnership and grow users by 500 percent in the next two years?*

"Holmes" was Danley-Ross' VP of community, Thad Holmes; he was one of the people who had pooh-poohed the earlier list of ideas from the initial meeting. "I'm not clear as to why we have to dedicate more resources to bolster this specific partnership when we already have several going on," he had said.

When we learned this, we said, "What about Holmes? Since he was challenging your ideas, why don't you invite him to participate?"

And that's when everyone groaned.

Sasha explained, "Holmes is a traditionalist, cautious and skeptical about untested ideas. He's attached to how things have always been done, and he believes he's a good reflection of our members. For example, he doesn't personally like being bombarded with online ads so he believes digital marketing will likewise annoy our members. It was a big deal for us to get him to agree to putting a few simple ads on social media to see what would happen, and because that didn't move the needle, he's more skeptical about it than ever."

"So, he *has* changed his mind in the past?" one of us asked.

"Yes," she replied, hesitant. "But it takes a lot of work. Including him in the conversation will only slow things down, as we'll have to spend our time convincing him to accept anything that's out of the box."

At this point, Trent spoke up. "But Sasha, one of the main reasons why things stalled was because he wasn't onboard. We need either him or someone more senior than him bought into whatever ideas we come up with. If not, no matter how great our ideas are, they won't be put into action like last time."

"I can see that, but is he even going to want to come? He tends to be very wary about any change initiative that doesn't come from the top down," Sasha replied.

After a lot of back-and-forth, the group concluded that including Holmes was going to be necessary to amping up the partnership. To anticipate Holmes' questions and angst about new ideas, they decided to invite a few marketing consultants who could bolster the case for digital marketing with some hard facts. They also decided to invite a few other department heads within Living Well in order to "spread the word" about this partnership throughout the entire workforce.

Pablo

Pablo is the CEO of Doregan, a multinational consumer product goods company. It is a large, 40-year-old company that is struggling to be relevant amidst changing consumer preferences and buying habits.

Pablo was pacing, floating in and out of view while videoconferencing with us. We were meeting with his team to discuss who should be convened for two and a half days to tackle the question they had formulated: *What must we do now and over the next six to 18 months across the enterprise to make our products relevant again and drive double-digit growth while maintaining acceptable margins?*

"Let me think," Pablo said, "we have to invite some of the brand leaders, heads of the regions in North America, South America, Europe, and Asia, as well as strategy, sales, marketing, and supply chain. And maybe a few of our longtime suppliers, retail partners, e-commerce partners, and our marketing agencies."

"That's a good start," we responded, "But think also about the people who are interacting directly with customers or who are making the products. They will be key to execution."

"Reynolds," Pablo directed his attention to a man on his right, his chief of staff. "Let's put some of our manufacturers, plant employees, and frontline sales into the mix."

Reynolds took notes on a laptop and then looked up at the camera to say, "Looking at the 12 zones guide, don't we need more people who are in 'the market'? We could think about inviting some actual millennial customers, since that's a key demographic we're hoping to reach. Maybe reach out to a few social media influencers or bloggers."

Pablo nodded, "That's a good idea, although I think some people may feel nervous about opening up in front of outsiders, especially if they have a platform to write or tweet about us."

At that point Jan from legal interjected that they could probably take care of that through strong confidentiality agreements.

Tanya, the chief strategy officer, responded, "I think what's most important is to make sure that we get a good mix of the old guard and the new within our company—people who feel protective of the status quo and may even be negatively affected by the changes we want to make, and people who are believers in change and are okay with embracing new ideas. And, Pablo, you know I'm talking about people not just in middle management but also our executive team and possibly Meredith from our board."

Pablo responded, "You're right, mostly, except for involving Meredith. I'm not including board members."

Reynolds, the chief of staff, spoke. "You know that Craig is definitely going to want to be a part of this. He's been part of Doregan almost since Day One, he's still beloved, and if we're going to make any big changes, we need him on our side."

"Craig," Pablo turned to face the camera in order to explain things to us, "is one of our presidents. He's announced his retirement and is leaving in a year."

"And if we invite him," Tanya said, "you know he's going to butt heads immediately with Kim, our head of analytics, who we have to have there. She only talks in terms of numbers, and he only talks in terms of stories."

"Well," we started to say, before Pablo cut in to say, "Invite Craig."

"That reminds me," Tanya said, "remember when we had the corporate fund-raiser and five-mile run last year? Wasn't it Jamal in Chicago who raised the most money and got almost everyone in his office to participate?"

Reynolds nods, "Yes, he's a sales director. Not very senior, but he's very social and well liked; he's always talking during town halls and participating in corporate forums. He's the kind of person who can easily convince other people to get on board with whatever he believes in."

The invite list wasn't fully resolved during that meeting. It took two more conversations for Doregan to nail down who they wanted and to ensure they had a cross section of people from across the 12 zones while still respecting their self-imposed limit of 36 people.

CHAPTER 7

Step 4. Localize the Solvers

ALTHOUGH NEUROSCIENCE and psychology are revealing more insights about the social wiring of our brains, the idea that we are fundamentally "social beings" is an ancient one. In the fourth century BC, Aristotle wrote:

> "Man is by nature a social animal; an individual who is unsocial naturally and not accidentally is either beneath our notice or more than human."[1]

His prescient insights have been confirmed and further elaborated by current neuroscientists. As Daniel Goleman puts it: "Neuroscience

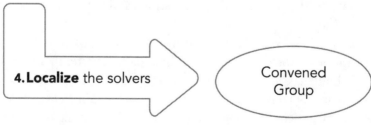

Figure 7-1   Step 4

has discovered that our brain's very design makes it sociable, inexorably drawn into an intimate brain-to-brain linkup whenever we engage with another person."[2]

We can verify through our experience that nothing—no current technology certainly—satisfies the very human need to get people into the room together if they're going to have any sort of substantive conversation. You can't, for example, deal with the "elephant in the room" without getting the elephant into the room.

As we make the argument about bringing people together in person, keep in mind that we're only talking about a few days (two or three). Is it really absolutely necessary for all of them to get together physically, especially when it's so easy to do virtually? A great deal of research has been done on the science of human connection and concludes that yes, it is necessary; it's not just our observations that fuel this step.

Nevertheless, we find it necessary to share some of this research because technology enthusiasts tend to more strongly and intuitively believe that virtual is as good as real.

The Value of Face-to-Face

Start by thinking about traditional snail-mail, email, or text—these communication platforms are great for talking *at* each other, for carefully thinking about what to say, checking and rechecking that you've expressed it well, keeping a record of what you said, and sending it only when you're sure you've nailed the message. But there's no real discourse, and there are no signals beyond the written word to discern tone, intention, or real meaning.

If you need a winking emoji to let someone know you're kidding, it's pretty obvious that you're dealing with stifled and potentially ambiguous communication.

Via telephone, you can discern more meaning in communication through tone of voice, hesitation, and words inadvertently blurted out without thought. Clearly, though, we're still missing body language and facial signals that convey so much emotion and meaning. Plus, there's the mute button, judiciously deployed to filter out the genuine reactions and commentary going on in each disparate room.

Figure 7-2 Elephant in the Room

So that's obvious: face-to-face clearly trumps no face at all.

Videoconferences are the answer, right? With that medium, you can hear voices, see faces, study body language (at least the parts that are visible on screen), and get the full picture. Right? No, not in our experience. There's more to communication than that, and there's much more to human connections than that. On top of these issues, technology can be plagued by bad connections.

We connect with each other in so many subtle ways when we're in the same place, and while it's hard to put your finger on exactly why, it's borne out in research.

In-person interactions, too, facilitate focus and a drive for results in a way that other mediums can't.

The Science of Human Connection

We are wired to connect. But not all types of social connections are equally impactful; some types matter more when it comes to effective problem solving.

The Natural Habitat

In 2012, psychologists led a research project to understand the impact that different meeting environments had on creative thinking.[3] They tasked pairs of participants with a problem to solve in 10 minutes (e.g., "Think of as many improvements to this product as you can"). They were divided into three conditions: face-to-face, videoconference, and phone. Each pair had to generate as many creative ideas or solutions as possible to the problem at hand. All pairs were evaluated on the number of ideas generated, the originality of ideas (how statistically infrequent they were), and the variety of ideas. The results? Overall, face-to-face pairs produced 30 percent more ideas than virtual pairs; their ideas were also moderately more original and diverse than virtual groups.

Two years later, a researcher at Northwestern University came to similar conclusions. Akshata Narain distributed a survey to people who work in face-to-face teams and people who work in virtual teams, asking them to rate how creative their teams were, to assess how frequently each team member expressed their thoughts, and how much team members' expertise and skills were utilized.[4] While some respondents suggested virtual settings reduced inhibitions for some when it comes to sharing information, overall face-to-face teams were rated more highly in terms of being creative, more communicative, and more fully engaging of each member's expertise and skills.

Why are in-person contexts more effective for group collaboration? A 2012 study conducted by researchers in Beijing Normal University may shed some insight. Researchers found that it's only when two people connect face-to-face that their brains experience "neural synchronization."[5] Participants who talked face-to-face experienced synchronized brain activity in the same area of their brains, which researchers believe resulted from the communication of "multimodal sensory information" (e.g., facial expressions, gestures) as well as more continuous turn-taking behaviors.

These results are significant in light of Google's massive, internal study of what distinguishes high-performing teams from low-performing ones: Not team cohesion, motivation, or average IQ, but rather frequent turn-taking in conversations and high social sensitivity toward what team members are thinking and feeling.[6] Pairing Google's insights with Beijing Normal's study, if face-to-face interactions indeed increase communication of multimodal sensory information—which will naturally help people become more socially sensitive to others—and promote turn-taking in conversations, then collaborating in person will inevitably have a positive impact on how groups perform and collaborate together.

The truth is that although much of our modern work experience is mediated through digital tools, our brains are still wired for face-to-face contact. Albert Mehrabian, a pioneer researcher of body language, found that when people communicate, the impact of a message is about 7 percent verbal, 38 percent vocal (e.g., tone of voice, inflection), and 55 percent nonverbal.[7] Communicating via technology, then, eliminates at least one, or even two, primary means that we use to convey our messages. Solving complex challenges requires bringing all the right people together, not for a virtual video conference but for a physical gathering. For only when we gather face-to-face can our beliefs, ideas, and feelings be fully conveyed and understood.

How to Localize the Solvers

Of all the 10 steps, this one is the simplest to understand: Bring everyone together.

Fast progress and mobilization requires face-to-face interaction. The requisite variety group must convene in the same place and sit in the room together or their collisions won't be effective. If they're not in each other's physical presence, they won't listen deeply and consistently, they won't get passionate about their beliefs, they won't challenge others with whom they disagree. If you believe in the importance of collisions, ask yourself if you can collide effectively with a group of other people by phone.

Our customers will either have the authority to tell people they have to participate, and they will come; or they won't have that authority, and they will have to convince them to come.

This is a large group of very important and very busy people, and you're asking them for two to three days of their focused and dedicated time. After your organization knows the Complexity Formula, it's much easier to convene a group. Until then, the three-day ask might feel like you're asking them for three months.

Making the Case for People's Time

If you have sufficient authority to make people clear their calendars, exert that authority.

Without authority, and without the support of those who do have the authority, you need to make the case for people's time.

There is no single right way to overcome a wide variety of legitimate reasons not to give you the time you're asking for. But here are some tips that can help counter objections you might hear:

Objection—Sorry, but . . .	Response
I'm not available on those dates.	If you can cancel those other commitments, please do. We will be working on one of the most important . . .
I can be there for some but not all of that time.	If the person who can't be there is key, you should have preempted that possibility by reaching out to them to determine their availability before finalizing dates. Otherwise, choose a best-possible substitute who can be fully committed.
I have more important places to be.	What could be more important than solving one of the most important challenges facing the organization? This will be a critical exercise and we need you there, working shoulder to shoulder with a bunch of other important and busy people. Here's who else will be there . . .

Objection—Sorry, but . . .	Response
I would prefer to join remotely.	Sorry, that won't work. We need you to be there in person. You'll understand why later.
I need to check with my boss.	Please do. And have your boss reach out to me if they're not sure about you coming.
I will need to get some other work done while I'm with you.	We'll help you work around a few interruptions here and there, but we need you there, in person and as focused as possible, for the entire duration.
Customer: Do you really need me there?	We hand-picked you as somebody who will really add important external perspectives / customer voice to what we're talking about. We need you there to keep us honest.
In any situation . . .	We will be working on one of the most important challenges facing the organization and you've been hand-picked to participate. Here's who else will be there . . .
With convening power . . .	Clear your calendar and be there.
In an organization that has used the Complexity Formula	Did you hear about the success we had applying this Formula to our \<growth in the oncology franchise\> challenge last year? We're doing the same thing now on \<cardiovascular\>. The results were amazing and we expect seriously important things to happen this time again.

These hooks can also help sweeten the pot for people:

- The **prestige** of being hand-picked to join this group and work on this challenge. Frontline people, for example, usually rejoice at being invited in to contribute to core challenges.
- The **names of others** who have already accepted.
- Cash **incentives**. In some cases, you may have to offer external people incentives to attend. Key professionals, like doctors, might require an honorarium, for example. An outside expert or consultant might require a fee.

The Payoff

At times, localizing people requires a strong push, and sometimes it's a no-brainer. In all cases, though, in retrospect, we're told that being in the same place was an essential factor to the success of the Formula. For example, we hear feedback that:

- We couldn't have turned around our stagnant service offering without getting everyone into the same room so they could get on the same page.
- The distrust between business and IT would never have been dissolved had we not convened together.
- The partnership (or integration) was floundering because we hadn't done a good job of getting everyone into the same room to straighten things out.

CHAPTER 8

Step 5. Eliminate the Noise

" **I** CAN'T HEAR MYSELF THINK," says the parent trying to concentrate in a house filled with screaming kids, music blaring, and the TV news anchor droning on about what's going on in the world.

"Why are you asking me?" asks your spouse when you're asking them for an opinion without nearly enough context or information to form an intelligent one.

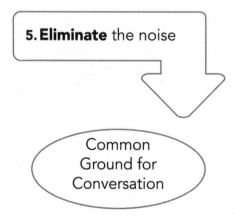

Figure 8-1   Step 5

"But it says so on the internet," says the embarrassed teen after citing a fact he's discovered and embraced before later finding out he's been completely misguided by an unreliable site.

The noise we're talking about in this chapter takes all forms—too much information all at once; too much wrong or inaccurate information; and too much missing, ambiguous, unreliable, or fragmented information. That's a disorienting mix of TMI, TMWI, and TMMI.

Knowledge Isn't Power

Today's leaders are receiving a constant stream of high-volume data and knowledge through various technologies, with little ability to separate between what matters and what doesn't matter, what's reliable and what's not reliable, and what's raw and what's processed. They are also dealing with inconsistent access to information and are often disconnected from the key information they need.

The noise we're talking about is all of the above.

When life was simpler, one of the characteristic challenges for organizations was *not enough* data, information, or knowledge. We were living in the time of "knowledge is power," and whoever had the best possessed a tremendous advantage.

Then we entered the information age, and everything changed as computers arrived and became ubiquitous, and with them data and information. Fast forward to today, when there is much more of a level playing field, with nearly equal access to data, information, and knowledge. There is so much of it, and it's so broadly available, that it's no longer power.

Power now lies in the ability to find meaning in the noise, to cut through it, and ascend the data-information-knowledge-understanding-wisdom hierarchy that we introduced earlier.

How to Eliminate the Noise

There are two levers to pull in this step. One is to provide people with baseline data, information, and knowledge. The other is to equip them to enter each other's world of language by diligently paying down the cost of codification with what may be perceived at first as halting progress.

Remember the context for this step from prior chapters: We are making our way toward clarity and action in the face of complexity. To recap, that means (so far) acknowledging it; developing a really good question that expresses the challenge; selecting the requisite variety of people to deal with it; and bringing them together for a brief and focused period of time.

While there, they will search for signals in the noise, fill in blanks for each other, and jointly move from what they know (the baseline facts; the data, information, and knowledge they each carry with them) to shared understanding.

None of that will happen if they can't "hear themselves think" because there is:

- Too little common ground regarding "the givens"/basic facts (generating noise as the group spins their wheels on things that could have been handed to them);
- Too much unfiltered and unreliable data, information, and knowledge;
- Too many language barriers and too little time spent crossing them.

As reported in CNN in September 1999, "NASA lost a $125 million Mars orbiter because a Lockheed Martin engineering team used English units of measurement while the agency's team used the more conventional metric system for a key spacecraft operation."[1] An extreme, oversimplified example for sure—but think of all the noise both teams were dealing with that prevented them from aligning on something as basic as "units of measure."

So how do you address these issues?

Too Little Common Ground

Whenever we bring together a high-variety group, there's always a great deal of surprise about how much basic information people *don't* have—about the organization, the market, each other's jobs, etc. We all have our heads down doing important work, and not everyone can keep up with the basics beyond the task in front of them.

And because the high-variety group often contains a few outsiders, they *really* don't know the basics that others might.

Apply rigor to level the playing field; make sure everyone is starting with the same basic information. Your challenge: separating fact from noise, bias, or opinion. Less is more. Whatever is missed in a preread or opening presentation can be filled in either through the conversations or by injecting missing facts later in other ways.

Still, make the "less-is-more" determination after you've thought about what should be shared.

What Information to Convey

First, go back to the really, really good question in step 2. The question provides a basic scope for the information to convey, and everything outside that scope is noise.

Now go back to the 12 zones of variety from step 3 for a moment. Use the picture below to remind yourself where people are coming from and why you've asked them to join the group.

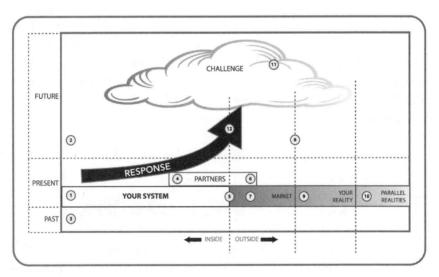

Figure 8-2   Challenge Cloud

Now ask yourself what the basic facts are that they might need to work with from each of the following zones.

Zone	Might Be Important to Share
1. Your System	• Operational facts and basic data about the system (size, revenue, org chart, etc.)
2. The (System's) Future	• Mission, vision, purpose, values, goals, objectives
3. The (System's) Past	• Current strategy, past strategies
	• A good glossary of terminology and acronyms
7. The Market	• Basic data and information about the market: The usual market research stuff—customer survey results, customer preferences, a good article about market trends, competitive analysis, strengths/weaknesses/opportunities/threats (SWOT), etc.
9. Your Reality	• Basic data and information about the industry and the environment: environmental scan, a good article
10. Parallel Realities	• Case study
11. The Challenge	• The latest data on the size, scope, and impact of the challenge; a good infographic or article
	• What customers, partners, and experts are saying related to the challenge
	• What projects/initiatives are already underway or planned related to this challenge
	• Why the group is being brought together to talk about it

The danger: sharing what you perceive as basic data, information, and knowledge that is actually opinion, unrecognized bias, or previous choices (that could well be wrong). For example, offering a customer relationship management piece full of great statistics compiled and authored by a specific technology vendor, or sending out the first draft of this year's brand strategy, may steer people toward the wrong answers instead of letting them find the right conclusions on their own.

Better to err on the side of sharing less if you're unsure. And once again, because it's hard for you to detect when you're introducing unintended bias, just as with your question, you should ask someone else to check for that.

Consider the job as doing the basic "discovery" for your group, without introducing bias. Save them some time—but let them discover everything else as they engage with each other.

At this point you've done what you can to reduce the noise. You gave them a question with clear scope, you've done your best to share the basic information, and you've brought all the right people into the room.

Beyond Prereads and PowerPoint Slides

It's not just about handing out information fact sheets. All sorts of ways exist to create a common knowledge base and to get people ready.

For example, you can provoke them to make them realize the urgency of the situation using a crisis scenario.

The CEO of a health organization that applied the Formula to accelerate the development of a pandemic plan needed to convey to her group just how fast their system would grind to a halt if unprepared for this emergency—but not unlikely—scenario. She did so by working with a few experts ahead of time to flesh out a chilling and realistic narrative that told of the exponential spread of an infection first appearing at a business conference in Asia and becoming a global pandemic in less than six weeks.

The scenario was brought to life through pictures and a ticking clock that gave the group the jolt they needed to dig into subjects necessary to address the situation. They were shocked at how

quickly the situation would ratchet out of control, all the precari-
ous dependencies they have on people being able to work together
face-to-face, and the sheer volume of cases they would have to
handle if this theoretical crisis ever became real. They responded by
creating an international gold-standard plan in less than two weeks.

Or you can use humor to have them see the need to change the status quo
differently by poking fun at some sacred cows in a short film.

An executive used a very funny, frank, and embarrassing video
showing customer perceptions about the industry to open a conversation on "Industry 2.0." The video included how fine print hides
details, the mismatch between over-the-top promises and actual
products, and the nightmare customer experience that is all too
common. Participants laughed at the industry while at the same
time feeling put off and a little shamed since they *are* the industry.

Or you can shift them from a potentially theoretical discussion to an
emotional one by having a dissatisfied customer or untreated patient tell
a story. (See Alicia's story at the end of this chapter.)

We've seen all three approaches work well, but don't limit your thinking to these three only.

Too Much Is Unfiltered and Unreliable

The value of your requisite variety group is that they themselves have
been accessing and processing the data, information, and knowledge
that's out there for years. It's their perspectives on what it all means that
you care about. Noise will crush and confuse them; they need space to
think.

In preparation for getting people together, we're often asked, "What
about the research? How will people know what's what if we don't do
the research first?" Sometimes, there's some research necessary and our

advice is to get it done fast and prepare a simple-to-digest report for the group—that's all. If it's not fast, it'll be too late. If it's not simple to digest, it'll be noise.

In conversations, one of the most common ways people retreat from boldness or defer work/thinking is by calling for *research*: "We need to study and analyze this. We need to launch an investigation. We need more data!"

Our response is (usually) to discourage recommendations that point to further research and instead ask the group to trust the tacit knowledge in the room and to guess what they'll find after a few months of research. Then, we tell them to state the assumptions behind the guess and move on.

One such time, in an environment heavy with the need for evidence, we had the group taking best guesses on several fronts, stating assumptions and making recommendations accordingly. The CEO then put the burden of proof in rejecting any of those recommendations on the research teams that were tasked with gathering the necessary evidence.

Recommendations didn't have to be proven right; they had to be proven wrong if they were to be removed from plan. We heard a few months later that none of the recommendations had been proven wrong.

Some mistakes may have been made. But when you're dealing with complexity you need to decide fast, act fast, and—if it turns out you were wrong—fail fast, learn, and keep going. Months and months of painstaking research can't keep up with a world that's changing by the week.

Err on the side of too little research, too little data, information, and knowledge—invest the effort instead in the requisite variety of people who carry the tacit data banks and the powerful processors around between their two ears.

Too Many Language Barriers

Having faith in the human beings and their tacit knowledge, hearts, and minds means they must be effective in their interactions with each other. They don't need to come in speaking the same language (because that's part of building shared understanding), but they do need to quickly get to a point where they understand each other's meaning.

Talk Isn't Cheap: The Cost of Codification

Dave Snowden, a Welsh management consultant and researcher best known for the development of the Cynefin framework, talks about the cost of codification in his blog here: http://cognitive-edge.com/blog/part-one-origins-of-cynefin/.

Cost of codification is crucial for grasping how high-variety groups move from data, information, and knowledge to shared understanding.

Essentially, Snowden makes the point that it costs a lot more in money, time, and effort to share knowledge with a large and diverse group of people than it does at the other extreme—amongst a highly homogeneous group.

We refer to the cost of codification as a "tax" that must be paid for effective communication. If you've done justice to requisite variety, then you're bringing together people from a wide variety of backgrounds and with a wide variety of expertise—the opposite of a homogeneous group. They all speak different languages—not literally (although sometimes), but conceptually.

If they were all mechanical engineers who work in the same office on the same projects and have been with your organization for 25 years, they would all more or less speak the same language. If one of them talked about the "damping ratio," everyone else would know exactly what he or she meant. Others would need to look the word up.

You get the idea. The cost of codification is a tax that you can't avoid. Unfortunately it is often overlooked, and you've probably seen it happen: Two teams or leaders agreeing on something but not aligned on the words used to describe it. In a recent great example, we observed a small group agreeing to protect "the global commons," and when we later asked the nonacademics in the group what that meant, they had no idea.

The important takeaway is that the cost of codification requires payment, normally takes a long time to pay down, and isn't something you can avoid. Just like any good tax. The Complexity Formula has the cost of codification baked into it and pays it down very quickly. We'll show you that in subsequent steps.

Alicia

Alicia is mental health director at Micbern, a large health system in the Southwest with a network of healthcare facilities and affiliated universities. It is working to mobilize organizations and institutions throughout the state to tackle the mental health crisis.

Alicia looked at the attendee list and did a double take. "I didn't know all these people were going to show up," she said to us.

On the list were some of the usual players: psychiatrists, nurses, primary care physicians, emergency room doctors, social workers, addiction specialists, and medical and nursing school professors, all of them from within Micbern's health system. But on the list also were representatives from patient advocacy groups, pharmaceutical companies, payers, treatment facilities, homeless shelters, nursing facilities, K-12 education professionals, prison medical directors, law enforcement, judges, and a handful of representatives from smaller hospitals and clinics located in suburban and rural areas of the state. They were all gathering for three days to answer the question: *What do we (all of us in the room) need to do individually and together in order to drastically turn the tide of our state's mental health crisis in the next two years?*

"To be honest," she said, "I'm surprised that these suburban and rural hospitals and clinics are showing up, given that they've traditionally grumbled at how we take their best doctors away from them, and even some patients."

We determined with her that the 43 people on the list were unlikely to read anything before the event. So if she was going to try to get people basic information, she would have to do so through an opening presentation when everyone was physically present in the same room.

"Where do I even start with trying to get people the basics that they need to know?" Alicia asked, perusing the list one more time. "Almost everyone here comes from a different point of view. And I don't want to rattle off a bunch of statistics about the mental health crisis in our state; everyone knows how dire things are."

We suggested she find a patient story that gets at the complexity of the crisis, one that illustrates how different institutions in her state must work together to best serve the patient.

After spending a few weeks asking around within the hospital and hearing a bunch of stories, Alicia finally found out about Raymond.[2]

Raymond was an 18-year-old who was living with his parents, Steve and Marcella, in the suburbs. He was very social and showed much more interest in talking and getting to know people than studying and reading for school. He was nevertheless on track to finish high school, but he had to take time off in his senior year due to escalating behavioral problems that his teachers didn't know how to handle. His bright, friendly demeanor was now punctuated with episodes of irritability, withdrawal, and disorganized behavior. On the recommendation of the school nurse, Steve and Marcella took him to a psychiatrist, who diagnosed him with schizoaffective disorder. Raymond took medication at his parents' request, but after some time he quietly stopped taking it, as he wasn't convinced of the diagnosis.

One night, after being out drinking with his crew of friends, he returned home and started acting in an irritated and impulsive manner. After some time, he grabbed a knife from the kitchen and started pointing it in several directions, including toward his mom. Steve tried to calm him down. It wasn't working, so he decided to call the police for help. The two officers who arrived had little training in dealing with people with mental illness; their loud, aggressive voices and movements scared Raymond, who started to frenetically resist their efforts to restrain him.

Luckily, a third officer arrived who had some experience with these situations, and he managed to de-escalate things. Marcella pleaded with the officers not to arrest her son. She knew that if he was arrested, she and her husband likely would not be able to come up with bail. Raymond would have to remain in custody without access to medication or any mental health support. Then the court would likely evaluate him as "incompetent to stand trial" and would require him to be "restored to competency" by a state hospital before trial. But if there weren't any available beds in the hospital, then Raymond would have to wait in jail until a bed opened up, and she had heard stories of how people like Raymond were treated in jail.

The third officer agreed with Marcella and convinced everyone to transport him to Micbern's psychiatric emergency room. There, after a long wait, he was evaluated and hospitalized overnight. The next morning, Raymond was much more stable, but the psychiatrist determined that he needed additional treatment and monitoring. There were no more beds left in Micbern's psychiatric department. A social worker called up a few residential treatment clinics nearby, but they were also at capacity. Finally, the social worker located a smaller hospital with a few extra beds, but it was a four-hour drive away. Steve and Marcella decided that it was not worth it given Raymond's stable behavior, so they took him home. The social worker gave them the phone number of a mental health response team to call in case something happened again.

Two months later, Raymond was showing signs of another episode. Steve was about to call the police but then he remembered the number that was given to him. The team showed up and managed to engage Raymond before his behavior escalated. They took him to a treatment clinic where he was able to stay for two weeks and interact with psychiatrists, occupational therapists, and social workers on a daily basis. At the clinic, he joined peer groups and met other people around his age who were on similar journeys. There, he worked with a social worker to set goals, get into a routine for taking medication, and better understand the triggers that upset him. After his time in the clinic, he moved back with his parents and entered a program targeted toward training people with mental health issues for employment. Through the program, he landed a retail job and found the support he needed to finish high school and attain a G.E.D. He moved out of his parents' home and into a house with friends from peer groups. One of Micbern's psychiatric nurses heard him tell his story at a local community center's fund-raiser for mental health, and so he told Alicia about Raymond.

When Alicia heard about Raymond's story, she knew that she would do whatever she could to get him to join the three-day gathering. After getting all the approvals she needed, she reached out to Raymond, who agreed to come.

When they convened a few weeks later, Alicia stood up to explain the purpose of the gathering, described the question that everyone was there to answer, and then turned the floor over to Raymond. Raymond spoke simply and clearly for 17 minutes, making eye contact with everyone in the room. He told his story as it began a few years ago but also about where he was today; how his medication had positively affected him; and how happy he was to sustain a relationship with his family and friends, to hold down a job, and to volunteer in meaningful ways. He also brought up a few concerns he had. His mental health treatment was covered through the Medicaid expansion, and he was concerned that the funding would be taken away, as his schizoaffective disorder counted as a preexisting condition, one that would likely affect what kind of private insurance was available to him. He also talked about the stigma of mental illness and how the stereotype of a violent, crazy person can rob those with mental health issues of any meaningful prospects. "Someone with an untreated mental illness is 16 times more likely to be killed by police than other civilians approached or stopped by law enforcement,[3]" he explained, "which is why I am so glad and lucky to be standing here in front of you, alive and well."

After he was finished, the room was silent. Everyone was taking the time to truly process his story.

CHAPTER 9

Step 6. Agree on the Right Agenda

B Y DEFINITION, complexity is multifaceted and entangled, and a requisite variety of people makes the best group to take on the job of figuring things out. But where do they start? How do they talk about something that is potentially an amorphous mess? Surely they need an agenda?

In fact, the opposite is true. Do not predetermine the agenda.

It may not sound like much, but this is a profoundly important and differentiated step in the approach to complexity. People will generally be surprised by the variety of people you have invited to a "conference," but they will be blown away when they discover there is no agenda. Even more, they will be astounded at how much of their time together is used to set the right agenda. That's Einstein's 55 minutes all over again. To find the order in complexity, the group first needs to order how they will approach it together.

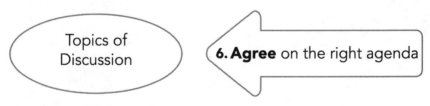

Figure 9.1   Step 6

Start by Deciding What to Talk About

Now that you've got all the right people focused on answering the really good question you've articulated, don't tell them what to talk about. If you were worried about introducing bias when you developed your question or decided what information to send out ahead of time, setting the agenda for the group will bias the outcome for sure.

Let the group decide what they have to talk about in order to answer the question. They need an agenda, and they need to be the people who set it. Their first task together is agreeing on how to deconstruct the question into the right component parts to discuss. This is the start of the "disentangling" of complexity we referred to earlier. What are the facets? What are the dots? How do we get at this? This is also when they begin to take ownership of the outcomes.

In our application of the Complexity Formula, we devote the first half day to agenda setting. That's how important it is.

Take a glance back at the 12 zones of variety again. That's a lot of ground to cover and a lot of disparate people who cover it. There's also a lot of data, information, and knowledge to deal with. And a bunch of language barriers to overcome. We have found that there is no better way to get started on the path to shared understanding than to first come to a shared understanding of the topics to cover.

It is also an opportunity to engage participants in something different and to get them owning everything that they will discuss and take with them after the Formula is completed. A certain mystique emerges when groups create their own agenda: It opens their eyes and minds to the possibility that their time together isn't going to be what they're used to. After they've completed the Formula, people reflect on the agenda-setting exercise as one of several pivotal moments in cracking the complexity.

If the challenge at hand is revenue growth, the span of potential topics could include:

- What is the envisioned future for the organization when it comes to markets and products? Where should we be seeking growth?

- What will be the impact of the planned growth on people in the organization? Are they equipped to deal with it? Are they incented properly?
- How will we fend off the current and emerging competitive threats so that we're not losing ground at the same time that we're trying to grow?
- Are our business processes scalable? Our technology infrastructure? Or does the planned growth overtax what we've got in place, and if so what do we do about that?
- What do our customers want and need from us? How will their demand fuel our growth?
- How will our culture be impacted as we grow? Do we have a culture that is able to adopt a growth mind-set?
- Are we innovative enough to develop the new products and services that will drive growth? Do we acquire innovations instead?
- Are there new markets that we need to go after? Should we be investing more in other countries and regions?
- And so on.

If the challenge is the threat of Amazon to the current business model, the group could need to talk about:

- Pricing strategy;
- Digitization and online presence;
- How we compete in emerging marketplaces;
- Regional and global disparities;
- Potential partnerships;
- Brand awareness;
- Efficiency in the supply chain;
- And so on.

The point isn't the list of topics above; the point is that nobody knows what all those topics should be except the requisite variety group.

Long after our customers have acknowledged their complexity and embraced a new approach, they have to come to grips with letting go of the reins they usually hold, and that starts with letting their group set the agenda.

I Know What They Need to Discuss. Why Waste The Time?

Be aware that even if you can accurately predict 70–80 percent of the topics, you shouldn't set the agenda; you are unable to create an agenda rich in ideas that are ideal for dealing with complexity. A diverse group can. They attach meaning, they choose, and they own.

The Curse of the Preset Agenda

What happens if you ignore our advice above and preset the agenda? You'll undermine the group's ownership and disempower them. You'll

Figure 9-2   Staff Meeting Minutes

also take a misguided step toward preanswering the question for them. You've intentionally or unintentionally (doesn't matter which) controlled the outcome. Stafford Beer said: *"When you preset the agenda and put it in a certain order, a good secretary can write the minutes before the meeting is held."*[1]

C. Otto Scharmer says: "Energy follows attention. Wherever you place your attention, that is where the energy of the system will go."[2] So, it's important to put everyone's attention on the right facets of the challenge. And you yourself can't possibly know what those are in total, when dealing with complexity—that's why you identified the talent you did. Only they collectively know the facets they need to cover.

So that makes it a wildly personalized set of topics, right? Every group is different. Every context is different. Every challenge is different. Or is it?

The Genetic Code of Complex Challenges

Complex challenges, like people, are very different on the surface, but share a common genetic code.

Think of your challenge as if it were a dot-to-dot puzzle. You see only a very small number of dots, but your requisite variety group should collectively have a sense of what most of the dots are. The problem: Each person sees only some and usually in isolation from all the other dots. Each individual fails to see the interconnections and interdependencies. The dots aren't numbered, so there's no obvious sequence. And the answer isn't known, so there's no picture to guess at.

In setting their own agenda, your group has taken the first step toward solving the puzzle. Many of the dots have been revealed, as well as some of the connections. They are ready to look for answers, to draw order out of disorder. They wouldn't be able to do this if there wasn't order to be found. Complexity is not the absence of order, it's just the absence of predictable, foreseeable order.

We have discovered an underlying order that has emerged for us over the years across a span of industries, countries, challenge types, questions, and groups. It is an order that emerges in the topics groups choose to discuss in addressing their complexity.

When we use the Complexity Formula with different groups, participants identify up to a dozen topics that they believe need to be addressed in order to tackle the complex problem at hand. You'd expect—as we did when we first studied this—this would mean hundreds or maybe thousands of different topics in aggregate across myriad industries and challenge types.

As it turns out, these groups propose and choose topics from only 23 subject areas. In fact, this is so consistent that we were able to create a tool that, based on answers to about 50 questions, can accurately predict what they will choose.

Think about that: Given a completely blank slate full of possibilities, any group from any industry or sector with any complex challenge will, over and over again, generate topics from *only* 23 subject areas. We call these subject areas the Genetic Code of Complex Challenges.

If you look hard enough, you can find "simplicity on the other side of complexity," as Oliver Wendell Holmes Jr. said. Our human bodies are incredibly complex; they are made up of trillions of cells that come with a complete set of instructions—made up of DNA—for making us who we are. It is, in some ways, astounding that all human DNA, no matter what the cell or body, is largely constituted out of a set number of chromosomes: 23 pairs.

No matter how complex the challenge, it will rarely veer outside of the confines of these 23 subject areas—they are the simplicity on the other side of complexity.

#	Subject Areas	Subtopic Examples
1	Who we are	Mission/Vision/Purpose, Brands, Values, Principles, Culture, Social Responsibility
2	Governance	Org Structure, Roles, Rules, How Decisions Are Made, Accountabilities/Ownership
3	Our People / Human Capital	Development, Compensation, Recruitment, Retention, Communication, Engagement

#	Subject Areas	Subtopic Examples
4	Results Management	Outcomes, Key Indicators, Reporting, Measuring Results
5	Internal Economy	Resource Allocation, Budgeting, Stability, Sustainability, Funding, Relationship with Global
6	How We Work / Core Processes	Internal Collaboration (Depts., BUs, Products, etc.), Core Business Processes, Lean
7	Information / Information Technology	IT Systems, Big Data, Knowledge Management, Best-Practice Sharing, Customer Information
8	Support Processes / Functions	Finance, Legal, Standards, Ethics, Risk Management, etc.
9	Bricks and Mortar / Infrastructure	Where Services Are Delivered, Workplace
10	Long-term Direction Setting & Adaptation	Strategy, Commitment to Change, Change Management, Leadership Development
11	Project Execution/ Implementation	Barriers, Enablers, Capabilities, Plan Implementation Details
12	Product / Service Innovation	Research, Development, Innovation
13	Understanding the Market	Market Research, Competitive Intelligence, Segmentation
14	Preparing the Market	Marketing, Advertising/PR/Promotion, Public Education, Image, Value Proposition
15	Key Partners / Supply Chain	Suppliers, Channels, Networking, Stakeholder Engagement, Labor Relations, Advocacy

#	Subject Areas	Subtopic Examples
16	Products and Services Quality	Standards, Guidelines, Quality Control, Safety
17	Sales	Sales, Sales Effectiveness, Sales Strategies / Tactics, Targeting, the Competition
18	Collaboration for the Common Good	Collaboration / Joint Projects between Orgs, Depts., BUs, Products, etc.
19	Customer Experience with Products and Services	Customer Experience, Service Delivery/ Support, Pricing, Access, Issues with Specific Populations
20	Customer Relationships	Alignment with Needs, Value Creation, Engagement, CRM, Account Management
21	Governance of the Environment	Governance, Policy, Regulation, Funding, Compliance
22	Changes in the Environment	Emerging Threats, Surveillance
23	The Customer Reality	How Customers Work, What Customers Need and Want, Changing Customer Demographics

Think of the Genetic Code of Complex Challenges as the landscape of subjects your requisite variety group might need to cover.

How to Set the Agenda

Start with individual brainstorming, move into clustering, then group clusters into possible topics, then decide as a group how to combine them (or in some cases drop some of them) to arrive at the final list for the agenda. It will take three to four hours to get this right.

Despite how simple that may sound, take a look at what's going on in each of those steps:

Individual Brainstorming

People have just shown up, having done their prereading on baseline information (maybe); listened to an opening presentation or two; been reminded of the really, really good question; and been introduced to a bunch of people who have been convened to answer that question (only some of whom they know), and they have no idea what topics they're going to discuss.

At that moment, we give them a few minutes to gather their thoughts. And not just gather them; record them. Why? They are each part of requisite variety, which means each has come in with a distinct point of view, set of experiences, stake, attitude, domain understanding, specialty, personality, processing capability, etc. If we immediately unleash them on each other, we lose the variety of what they came in with.

So the first step is to ask them to quietly reflect on the question and document their thoughts: ideas, concerns, lessons learned, stories, etc.

Clustering

They next post their anonymous thoughts in full view of everyone, then read what everyone else has to say. Here we have them scanning for thematic connections and duplicates, and moving them together into clusters. The clustering isn't really the point yet; it's more about giving people time to see what is on everyone else's mind, the language they're using, their attitudes, and their ideas.

It also helps organize the content a bit and get people ready to start forming possible topics.

Clustering the Clusters

Now we have them look for compelling topics to be considered for the final agenda. Everybody's free to suggest as many as they want, and everybody's free to agree or disagree with what others are suggesting. If enough people agree, a topic makes the short list. If not, it's politely set aside.

Finalizing the Agenda

With a short list of possible topics identified, the group is now given a set number of topics to arrive at and a finite amount of time to do so. They are also given someone to record their recommendations.

Topics that are similar are merged, or in some cases one swallows another. Some topics are dismissed as being out of scope or unimportant. Some topics point to guiding principles that don't need discussion at all.

At the end, the right number of topics stand, and everyone knows why they made the list, what they contain, and what outcome they will be trying to produce.

This is one way to go about forming the agenda. There are others. If you're building your own, look for these characteristics:

- Everybody can contribute their own content before dealing with the content of others;
- Everybody has an equal say in what is and isn't on the agenda;
- Topics are filtered based on how important *and* interesting they are;
- The exercise is engaging and sets the right tone;
- It leads to shared understanding with respect to what's on the agenda—why chosen, why important, how it's meant to contribute to answering the overall question.

Good and Bad Topics—and How to Tell the Difference

Here are some lessons we've learned over time about good topics for discussion. We've also learned how to ask the convened group the right questions, so they can assess whether a given topic can be categorized as *good*:

Characteristics of a Good Topic	Prompts to Test for This
Interesting to almost everyone	How many of you would rank this in your top three once we have 12 topics?
Undeniably relevant to the question	Can somebody state a goal that reflects our overarching question through the lens of this topic?

Characteristics of a Good Topic	Prompts to Test for This
Holds the promise for some actionable recommendations	What's an example of an action that might come out of this discussion?
Reflective of some strand of the complexity being faced	How does this topic contribute to the complexity in the question?
Important to resolve	What's at stake if we don't resolve this?

And here are some topics to be careful with:

- Culture. People want to tackle culture, but it's tough to find actionable recommendations because culture is usually affected by other things and tough to affect head-on. When the topic is broadly about culture, our experience is that wheels spin but little traction is found. If the topic can get more specific about a cultural barrier to be addressed—like risk aversion or growth mindset—then it's much easier for the group to talk about the 'how' and find traction.

- Any topic where there is little control to be wielded by the group. For example, a topic that will lead to recommendations about a project or program that isn't represented in the room can easily be a waste of time.

- Leadership. It's always uncomfortable for nonleaders to identify these topics because of power dynamics. We pay special attention to leadership topics for this reason and push harder than usual for people to get past the discomfort and get real with their recommendations.

People are used to arriving at meetings and reading through a pre-set agenda. By turning the agenda over to them, you set a different tone and you give them ownership. The agenda-setting exercise engages them, and they respond with some expected topics, some that surprise you, some straightforward ones, and some emotionally charged ones. The discussions about which topics to choose can become very heated—and that's great, because that demonstrates ownership and commitment.

Pablo

Pablo is the CEO of Doregan, a multinational consumer product goods company. It is a large, 40-year-old company that is struggling to be relevant amidst changing consumer preferences and buying habits.

Pablo was watching the room descend into controlled chaos before his eyes. Just 10 minutes ago, the entire room of 36 people was quietly listening to a short presentation on trends and stats about shifting consumer habits and new competitive threats, drilling home to everyone, especially the longtime employees, the urgency and necessity of change. And now, the room seemed to be taking on a life of its own.

Not only was the room so diverse that he didn't recognize half the people who were participating in the current exercise of agenda setting, but there were multiple pockets of conversation happening at once.

To his left, there were three people debating the quality of Doregan's personal care products. A senior VP blurted out, "Let's be real. I've stopped buying our brands." One of the older sales reps responded, "Are you kidding? I love our products."

The third person, who worked in finance, responded, "Regardless of who among us loves it, let's just keep in mind that most of our customers do. I know our products could be better, but we can't look down on our customers when, frankly, they're the ones who are paying us to be here right now."

To Pablo's right, there was a small huddle of people who led start-ups that Doregan had recently acquired. They sold natural and more sustainable home care products—directly to consumers—that competed, in some ways, with Doregan's brands. This group of people seemed to be standoffish and mostly talked to themselves.

"Doregan isn't even on the label of our products. It's in the fine print," one of them said, folding his arms across his chest. Tanya, the chief of strategy, was walking by and overheard what was said. She turned around and replied in her usual direct manner, "If Doregan thrives in the next decade, then we all, including all of you, will benefit. We're in the same boat."

Behind him was another conversation, this time on Doregan's digital and technology strategy. A young software developer was animatedly asking, "I just came back from a conference on the Internet of Things, and that's definitely the future of consumer goods—washing machines are already alerting people about low supplies and buying goods online by themselves. Do we even have a strategy for this?"

An account manager for retailers responded, "I don't know if we can compete there; I think we should focus more on retail customers. Retail is our bread and butter and I fear we're losing sight of that." A third person, who worked in data analytics, said, "The future is digital. We can't rely on retailers to connect with our customers; we need to connect with them directly on Instagram, online TV, Facebook, and maybe even start integrating them into our product-development cycles."

Pablo was taking in many of the conversations he was overhearing. He turned to us, asking, "There are so many things being discussed and I love the energy and buzz, but I'm worried if we can land this. Also, what if some topics that I really want to discuss don't make the cut? We only have two and a half days to discuss everything."

Just then the person running the exercise spoke up in a booming voice, "I see that many of you are having intense debates. I would encourage you to wrap it up if a conversation takes longer than five minutes. We're here to set the agenda, not to answer the question yet. So if a topic is provoking so much debate, it's probably worth putting it on the agenda so that you can continue the conversation for the next three days."

We turned to Pablo to say, "It feels chaotic, we know, as it always is. But this is how everything gets put on the table. And the next exercise will organize everything into topic clusters, and you'll see the patterns emerge—all the topics will fall into some of the 23 subject areas that we talked about last week. And the topics that are most relevant will make it into the final agenda. Please speak up if you feel strongly about certain topics."

After 15 more minutes of conversation, key topics from the room started to emerge on a short list: sustainability, emerging markets, next-gen customers, revitalizing the core, innovation agenda, adapting to channel complexity, etc.

Then the whole group sat down and spent another 45 minutes consolidating topics, eliminating topics and then deciding on the final list of 12 topics that would constitute their agenda for the rest of the three days. Sure enough, the topics that Pablo cared most about made it into the agenda without needing to push—along with a few others that he didn't expect at all.

Brenda

Brenda is SVP of finance at Plesius Finacorp, a financial services company that has a 10-year-old partnership with Danley-Ross HealthAge, a seniors association. The partnership has been vastly underperforming compared to its potential.

Brenda kicked off the gathering of 25 people with a short presentation that briefed everyone on the details of the current partnership between Danley-Ross and Plesius, the immense value proposition for Danley-Ross' members and the revenue opportunity for Plesius. Then Sasha came up to explain a bit more about Danley-Ross' culture and their approach to their network members for the benefit of Plesius' employees. Everyone went around the room to introduce themselves, including the two marketing consultants who were there to participate.

The first step in setting the agenda was to have everyone write down various statements, concerns, questions, etc., that they believed were relevant to answering the question *What can Danley-Ross HealthAge and Plesius Finacorp do to change the trajectory of our current partnership and grow users by 500 percent in the next two years?*

Then these anonymous notes were collected and displayed in a corner of the room for everyone to read and discuss. The energy in the room was a little low. A handful of the notes read, "Why am I only really learning about this partnership now?" But as people began to circulate and read the notes and riff on them, conversation started to pick up.

A community director at Danley-Ross walked up to Sasha, who over-saw corporate partnerships at Danley-Ross, and said, "The more I'm learn-ing about this partnership, the more I'm seeing the connections. Why don't we have a process set up to connect everyone who contacts us for financial advice with Plesius?"

Soon, the notes were organized into clusters and eventually turned into "topics" for the agenda. There were 21 topics proposed, and the room was tasked with boiling them down to just nine. Thad Holmes, Danley-Ross' VP of community who had decided to participate after some cajol-ing, was rather vocal in asking why targeted marketing deserved an entire topic. "Didn't we already try some ads that didn't work? Why do we need to have an entire discussion dedicated toward this, when everyone knows people over 50 aren't online?" he asked, leaning back in his chair.

Sasha responded, "Those ads weren't targeted, so only three out of 10 contacts we got were from members. We need more targeted outreach, and, Thad, last I read, more and more Boomers are active online."

One of the consultants in the room responded, "Did you target those ads toward people who have liked you on social media? That would limit the scope to people who are at least interested or fans of Danley-Ross."

A junior sales analyst at Danley-Ross gingerly raised his hand to say, "Maybe we shouldn't limit the scope, because opening it up may be a good way to get new people to sign up to be members of Danley-Ross, especially if we advertise to Plesius' network as well."

Someone at Plesius raised their hand and said, "We can definitely highlight our partnership with Danley-Ross as part of our marketing and recruitment of seniors. Maybe we should have a new topic that is about integrating this partnership into other departments and processes at Danley-Ross and maybe even Plesius. My group does estate planning, and I'd be open to talking to Danley-Ross to see if we could establish a partnership there too."

Thad responded swiftly, "Hang on, before we get too crazy, I want to make sure we maintain our respectful relationship with the community. Signing up with us is about joining a network, not putting your name on a mailing list. I was the one who proposed the topic on branding, and I feel strongly that this should be one of the agenda topics."

Then a VP who ran client services at Plesius spoke up. "Putting in my two cents here as a bit of an outsider, I think one of the reasons why the energy behind this partnership has been sluggish is because not everyone immediately understands the value of financial planning and investment. And sometime retirees feel real shame about not having enough savings, such that they don't want to open up their bank accounts to an outside professional. I think we should have a topic just on understanding and communicating the value of financial planning, especially for seniors."

As the conversation continued, Brenda turned to us to say, "I've heard many of these objections, concerns, and ideas before, but the amazing thing is that this conversation is being had across a wide network of people, and everyone gets to listen and respond. This is the most effort and energy I've seen all these people put into actively discussing this partnership—I'm usually trying to chase down all these people to give me 15 minutes of their time."

"But," she continued, "I'm worried that we won't have enough time— we only have two days—to solve some of the problems that have been raised."

We assured her that this is how most people feel after the agenda-setting exercise: Energized by the inputs from everyone and the discussion, but overwhelmed and confused as to how to proceed and doubtful about making headway.

"Wait until we split up into groups for each of the topics and start iterating," we told her. "You will see answers emerge—and some of them may even surprise you."

CHAPTER **10**

Step 7. Put People on a Collision Course

ETHAN ZUCKERMAN, American media scholar, blogger, and Internet activist, said: "Engineering serendipity is this idea that we can help people come across unexpected but helpful connections at a better than random rate. And in some ways, it's based on trying to reassess this notion of serendipitous as lucky—to think of serendipitous as smart."[1]

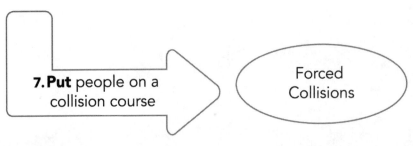

7. Put people on a collision course → Forced Collisions

Figure 10-1   Step 7

In the early days, we tried to explain to a very smart person what it is we do. His reaction: "Oh, I get it. You engineer serendipity." That's really stuck with us, so you might say it was a happy accident that we met him.

All these years later, we can say with certainty that serendipity can be engineered. Serendipity often happens where people, domains, and/ or systems collide. And collisions can be engineered.

With complexity's many moving parts, interconnected facets, unknowns and unknown unknowns, to make effective progress on a complex challenge requires new ideas, fresh insights, and unconventional strategies. Serendipitous breakthroughs are needed fast, and for that, you need engineering.

The question becomes how to engineer collisions so that they happen on purpose and so that smart serendipity happens.

Engineering Serendipity through Forced Collisions

First, what do we mean by collisions? People bumping into other people, talking directly to each other, listening to each other, then moving on to another collision. When we talk about domains and systems colliding, we mean people from one domain or system bumping into people from another domain or system.

These kinds of collisions generate sparks, whether sparks of conflict or sparks of harmony. New things happen when you put people together with those they haven't met before and when you put people together with ideas and perspectives they haven't heard before. For example:

- A payments company that was talking about the emergence of smart cards and how that was enabling new kinds of competitors in their market eventually identified two new product categories they could enter and quickly went from playing defense to playing offense. This breakthrough came as a result of the collisions we engineered for them between people from their core business and others not constrained in their thinking by the traditional business model.

Sometimes breakthrough ideas seem revolutionary, and sometimes they seem incremental, but big or small, they result from collisions between people who aren't ordinarily brought together.

How Many Collisions?

To engineer serendipity and leave little to chance, generate collisions between each pair of people in your requisite variety group. That means connecting everyone directly with everyone else. For eight people you would draw the picture of those connections like this:

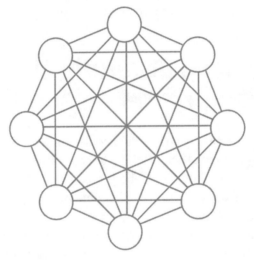

Figure 10-2   Connections

The number of connecting lines between those eight people, if you count them, is 28, or (8 x 7) / 2. That's the standard calculation for the number of connections among eight people when everyone is directly connected to everyone else. And that's 28 collisions to force in a group of eight.

In a group of eight, though, you don't really need to force anything: Gather them around a typical round banquet table and they can easily manage those 28 collisions themselves. That's why we call groups of eight or fewer people *collision teams*; that's the maximum number of people who can effectively interact amongst themselves without special effort.

Collision teams (of eight) don't constitute requisite variety, which, as we said earlier, is more likely to be somewhere between 20 and 50. Let's say it's 42 people, for example; then the number of *connections* amongst them is calculated as (42 x 41) / 2 = 861. At 50, the number is (50 x 49) / 2 = 1,225. Now you're into numbers that are much harder to manage—and that's just the number of connections. Each of those two-person connections, to achieve the results that we're looking for, will host multiple collisions between the pair as they talk, listen, argue, separate, come back together, and do it all again. If we're talking about 1,225 connections in total for the group, we're talking tens of thousands of collisions overall. Depending on the challenge and therefore the number of people who make up requisite variety, there can be as few as a thousand collisions to manage.

In every case, the question becomes, how do you force so many collisions? How do you make them meaningful? And how do you capture what happens at each collision point?

Let's look deeper at $n(n\text{-}1)$—also known as "n multiplied by n minus 1"—the basis for the above calculations.

The Collision Equation: N(N-1)

First of all, why $n(n\text{-}1)$ and not $(n(n\text{-}1))/2$ as we were using above? Why aren't we dividing by 2?

In the standard calculation for the number of connections amongst people, dividing by 2 prevents you from double-counting the connections. That's because when you're just looking at connectivity, Tom connected to Sally is the exact same thing as Sally connected to Tom.

When we talk about forcing collisions, we don't mean that a collision between Tom and Sally should necessarily be the same as the collision between Sally and Tom. Sometimes, the collision is set up in such a way that Tom is allowed to speak, and Sally is only allowed to listen. Other times, Tom is only allowed to listen while Sally speaks. Other times they're both speaking, and still other times, they're both listening.

We might actually force Tom and Sally to connect in four different ways, which means $n(n-1)$ actually undercounts the number of collisions. We'll keep it simple here, though, by using that formula.

If we arbitrarily set requisite variety at 42 people, how do you bring about the $n(n-1)$, or 1,722 collisions? Put them all around a table and have them talk it out? You already know that doesn't work.

How about interviewing everyone?

The Traditional Hub-and-Spoke Model

That's the traditional task force or consulting model for connecting people: the "hub-and-spoke." An individual or a small group of people (task force, outside consultants) reside at the hub of the effort and collect all information and knowledge relevant to the problem. The people being connected (e.g., from the organization) are positioned as the spokes, providing their needs, wants, and perspectives to the hub in interviews. The solving responsibility is given to those playing the starring role at the center.

This traditional approach works well when you are dealing with simple or complicated issues. In the installation of a new order-management system, for example, a team of experts/consultants is assigned to interview a cross section of the organization in order to custom-fit the same solution they've delivered many times before. They just need to gather requirements from the identified people (users, approvers, and so on), and then they have what they need to configure the solution.

When dealing with the complex, though, interviews and analysis aren't enough. The people at the hub are in over their heads. The job at hand isn't simply to configure a known solution; it's to figure out a new one. They have to deal with all the noise that each individual they interview is dealing with. They can only proceed linearly—step by step, interview by interview—so it takes too long. Silos don't get busted because only the hub is navigating them.

Most importantly, the interviewees aren't colliding with each other, only with the hub (and possibly the small number of others present with

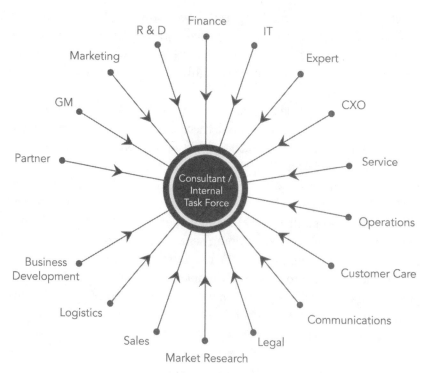

Figure 10-3   Hub-and-Spoke

them in the interview). The interviewees aren't reaching a shared understanding, only the people at the hub are—eventually. The interviewees aren't gaining clarity or cocreating a solution; it's being given back to them by the hub. Which means the ownership for the solution exists only at the hub.

And for all these reasons, execution suffers.

Nonetheless, when deployed on complex challenges, both task forces and consultants use the same expert-centric, hub-and-spoke model that they rightly apply to complicated challenges—and in doing so, they essentially ignore the material differences between complex and complicated.

We have been called into very large transformation projects in the months or years following the delivery of a solution by a traditional consulting firm. The transformation effort was massively complex, our customer had called in the consultants to develop a strategy and a plan, and they had delivered just that—a long time earlier. The solution had been developed using the hub-and-spoke: Many, many people had been interviewed, various iterations had happened with senior management, and ultimately a beautiful work product had been delivered. We don't mean that sarcastically; the strategy was highly regarded, it was smart, and it was probably right.

We were being called in, however, because in the months (or years) since, little was being implemented, there was resistance, people weren't doing what they were being asked to do, deadlines were being missed, and the original complex challenge was still festering.

People didn't *own* the strategy. They either didn't believe it was right, or they didn't understand it, or both. The consultants they had used were either long gone or still in there plugging away, trying to get people going: doing change management, helping senior leadership with persuasion campaigns, still trying to get to the heart of what was going on.

We helped them to apply the Complexity Formula on the execution challenge, and in all cases the same root cause emerged: people didn't believe in the strategy. Through the Formula, they were able to get all the right people together (including the consultants) to talk about how to move forward, to get their fingerprints on the strategy, to take ownership for it, and ultimately to get unstuck in execution.

This happened in financial services, with a bank trying to implement both customer-centricity and anti-money-laundering compliance at the same time; this happened with a pharmaceutical company trying to shift to an account-based go-to-market strategy; and this happened in several tech companies implementing software as a service (SaaS) while shaking up their portfolio of products.

In all these cases, the mistake was using the hub-and-spoke model to try to solve a complex challenge.

The Costs of Applying the Hub-and-Spoke Model to Complex Challenges

Here is a summary of what happens when the hub-and-spoke model is used on a complex challenge:

- It immerses the task force/outside consulting team (the hub) in a rich learning environment, when instead what's needed is shared learning and understanding across the organization.

- It places the onus on the task force/consulting team to somehow surface everything, do the thinking, and create a novel solution. The people at the hub will struggle for months to generate fresh answers and having done so, having created the solution instead of informing it, the result is a partial, "clinical" solution that won't be executed. Despite all the effort and potentially world-class solving, the hub won't be able to pass ownership to everyone else. Ownership is lodged in the center with the people who built and gradually came to believe in the solution, not with the organization's doers and leaders who will drag their feet to execute on the strategy.

- It ignores the need for thousands of collisions and settles instead for a few one-way encounters with each person. It is structurally set up for linear processing and thus is slow. The model moves interview by interview and document by document before putting the task force or consultants in a position to generate preliminary recommendations. If anything happens in parallel, it's a fluke in scheduling—it's not parallel processing. Which means it moves at a linear pace, an interview at a time, with long pauses in between for thinking and processing. By the time the solution has been developed, a lot has likely changed and new complexities have arisen.

- It treats change management as phase two. It usually ignores or deprioritizes engagement and mobilization—forces that are absolute prerequisites to the successful implementation of any solution—and introduces these elements after the fact (after the program has been developed). This means a persuasion campaign must be part of the equation—creating a plan to overcome organizational resistance because the employees and managers charged with implementing the task force/consultant program weren't involved in its creation. They will do what leaders require, but they will do it reluctantly, skeptically, uncreatively, and above all else, slowly. Another task force is often required to figure out how to ramp up implementation and engage your people.

- It skirts the "silos" issue by using the people at the hub as the emissaries crossing silos, rather than connecting silos directly to each other. Those at the hub meet with Business Unit A, then with Business Unit B, then with IT, then with HR, and so on (for example). The people in Business Unit A don't meet directly with those in Business Unit B, or IT, or HR, they meet with the hub. They don't collaborate across the silos in building a solution; they don't collaborate at all in this model. The result is that the silos are still comfortably standing when the consultation is done.

For all those reasons, even really good strategies, written by the best minds in the world via the hub-and-spoke, tend to gather dust on the shelf.

These disadvantages were problematic enough before; today, they're likely to be the critical factors leading to project or transformation failure. Organizations can no longer take months or longer to develop recommendations, followed by more months of planning, followed by months of mobilization and implementation. Business situations and market dynamics change faster than that.

Why Do Organizations Still Cling to This Model?

Organizations are still relying on this model for many reasons, including but not limited to:

Figure 10-4   Strategy Execution

- The myth of talent scarcity, which we discussed earlier;

- The attractiveness of outsourcing the solving to someone else, given scarce time and resources within the organization;

- The temptation to view complex challenges as boil-the-ocean challenges and the seeming attractiveness of hub-and-spoke, which tries to break challenges down into manageable but disconnected parts and avoids ocean boiling;

- Hub-and-spoke feels safer and demonstrates that you're working on it;

- There just hasn't been anything better.

The Model for Complexity: Many-to-Many

The only way to unlock the full power of n people is to use a many-to-many structure that connects each person effectively and fully with every other person in the group. Each person has their own individual pieces of the puzzle, but those pieces need to be assembled by them, not for them. This is the key to maximizing the value of requisite variety.

You saw a many-to-many picture earlier for eight people; Figure 10-5 shows what a many-to-many structure looks like with even more people.

Each line represents a connection between people, a channel through which they can collide and where serendipitous breakthroughs are possible: differentiated insights; hidden opportunities; bold new tactics; winning strategies.

Each of the n people is a hub with spokes that connect to each of the other n-1 people; in other words, there are n hub-and-spoke models all happening at once. There is no center. There is no dominant place in the network. Everybody creates, everybody owns.

To build this network, to generate the thousands of collisions that it forces, focus on four objectives:

- Ensure the connections enable robust, back-and-forth dialogue.
- Monitor and capture what happens over each connection.

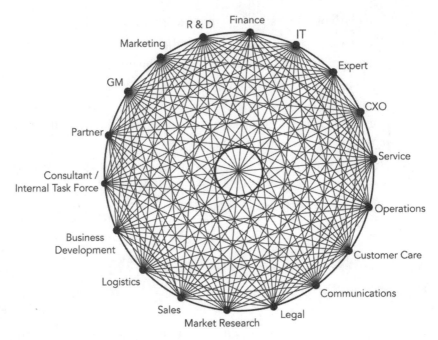

Figure 10-5   Many to Many

- Activate each connection repeatedly, so that every collision has a chance to inform and be informed by what's happening along every other connection and to benefit from the insights that are popping up everywhere.
- Ensure the connections are sustained.

Density of Variety

The *density of variety* metric makes the point about how important it is to sustain the connections once you've set up the many-to-many model to generate the n(n-1) collisions.

We define variety density as a measure of your success in convening requisite variety: when everyone needed is brought together, variety density is 100 percent; when nobody comes, variety density is 0 percent.

Variety density is calculated as *actual variety* divided by *requisite variety*, or $(m(m-1))/(n(n-1))$, where m is the number of people convened from amongst the n people who are required.

When one of the *n* people is removed, the *n*-1 collisions that person would have had with the rest of the group are lost, and variety density shrinks not just by one person, but by that person and all those collisions. When a second person is removed, variety density shrinks again, and the opportunity cost of less-than-requisite variety is increasing, not on a straight line, but on an exponential curve.

Let's look at an example:

- When requisite variety is 42 people for a given challenge, 42x41 is the number of connections to be managed, which is 1,722. When all 42 people are present, *m*=*n* and variety density is 100 percent.

- When one person is removed, you lose about 5 percent of your variety density. Lose another person and you're down about 10 percent; lose 12 and you're down about 50 percent. You still have 30 of 42 people participating, but you've lost half the variety density required for a successful outcome.

On a chart, it traces an exponential curve:

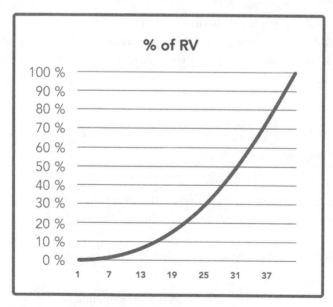

Figure 10-6 Exponential Curve

If the math doesn't do it for you, consider this analogy instead: *removing baking soda from a recipe has a much larger impact on the recipe than merely the absence of a single ingredient because of the chemical reactions that don't happen in its absence.* Remove a person from your requisite variety group, and you change the formulaic potential because you're also removing all the "chemical reactions" between them and others. Requisite variety isn't just about the individuals in isolation; it's about the potential of the group to reach "better than the sum of the parts" results because of the collisions and reactions amongst the individuals.

The bottom line is twofold:

- You've got to bring a requisite variety group together for the Complexity Formula to have full impact.
- Once together, you need to use a many-to-many network to connect them and to force collisions amongst them in order to engineer serendipitous breakthroughs. That means they need to remain together and engaged to get the full value of each individual and all those collisions.

When the requisite variety exercise identifies an individual who's a great fit in all respects but unable to be present the whole time, look for the "Plan B" person who can stay for the whole thing. A person can only be part of requisite variety and the many-to-many network when you actually have them.

How to Put People on a Collision Course

It's not just about *having* collisions. Effectively managing them requires deliberate engineering and careful orchestration. How?

- Set up the right many-to-many network model for the size of the group.
- Assign people to collision teams (where eight or fewer people are conversing at any given time) to discuss the topics they chose for the agenda.

- Connect the teams to each other so that across all the topics, everyone interacts with everyone else multiple times.

- Run through each topic three times, so that every collision team can inform and be informed by every other collision team (making sure that information flows from team to team via the people attending the meetings and written reports about what transpires in each room).

Putting people on a collision course comes down to establishing a sequence of small-group interactions that systematically put everyone in direct contact with everyone else multiple times.

A High-Efficiency Megabrain

Having structured people and topics in this way, each collision team will have many people's brains in it, and each of those brains will act like a neuron in a team brain addressing a topic. In turn, each collision team will act like a neuron in an $n(n-1)$ networked megabrain addressing the overall question.

Just like actual neurons firing in a brain, the conversations that are set up through the Complexity Formula create sparks, insights, clarity, questions, and answers that the many-to-many network transmits to everyone else.

Look at the many-to-many illustration again. Put your finger on one of those connecting lines and pretend something happens that's important on that line. Trace a direct path from that line to any other person in the network to see how many steps it takes.

A well-constructed many-to-many network is an efficient megabrain fueled by people and connections between people. It's hyperfast, it transmits what matters and filters out what doesn't, and it draws on the widest possible variety of people (representing the 12 zones and the 13 characteristics). The megabrain is at the heart of the Complexity Formula.

Whereas CEOs and other senior executives often feel like their people aren't on the same page or are communicating in disjointed, asynchronous ways, this step represents the ideal they aspire to—it creates the ultimate team, where diversity, cross-functional structures, and other team attributes are maximized.

Managing the Collisions

You will need to manage how and how often people interact within their collision teams to ensure best possible results, and we will give you additional instructions on how to do that in steps 8 and 9, using:

- Roles that drive robust and balanced back-and-forth dialogue;
- Mechanisms that monitor, capture, and quickly feed forward whatever happens in the room to the rest of the requisite variety group;
- Iteration, so that everyone can benefit from the insights that are popping up everywhere.

For now, though, remember that at the point where any two people collide as the Complexity Formula progresses, they already have some shared context:

- A connection to the complex challenge at hand, expressed in the question they've been convened to answer;
- Whatever level-setting prereads and presentations they've been exposed to;
- An agenda made up of topics they had a hand in cocreating;
- Conversations that have potentially already started on some or all of those topics.

And now they collide, in a small group meeting on some topic. Depending on the nature of their assignment in that room, each may be in a speaking or a listening role. What does that collision look like?

It looks like highly engaged, intense conversation.

They aren't exchanging notes, or writing/reading reports, or hugging, or engaging in a trust- or team-building exercise. They are having a conversation about the question and their specific topic related to that question, whether it's about incentives, or technology, or leadership.

There's nothing standing between the people in the room except a table. The note-taker in the room isn't standing between them. They're looking at each other, talking to each other, listening to each other, and reading each other's body language.

They talk. They argue. They tell stories. They teach each other and learn from each other. They share information. They ask and answer questions. They get frustrated with each other. Their brains are together in a natural habitat in which they can do their best work.

These collisions take many forms. A semiconductor manufacturer had convened 30 or so people to figure out how to make sure that its products were leading in the industry. There was a fairly quiet and introverted participant who was not a big talker during the group meetings, which were often fairly loud and rambunctious. Toward the end of the day, however, there was an exercise where each person got a chance to read the notes compiled from all the topic groups, including ones they were not a part of. There was no name or author attached to any of the text in the notes; participants were engaging directly with the ideas presented, not who was behind them.

Each topic group had a station with all the notes from their discussion taped onto it. After finishing reading the notes, participants wandered from station to station, providing their feedback on the notes. There would be one representative from the group standing at the station to explain any part of the notes, dialogue with people, and take in feedback.

The quiet participant came alive during this session, as she walked around to each station and engaged in one-on-one conversation with the sole presenter stationed at each station. The presenters later brought insightful feedback from her and many others back to their topic groups.

All the previous steps have taken the participants to this point where they can have a really good conversation. While they're together doing that, they don't have to notice or pay attention to what's going on around them (the many-to-many network, why and how they were chosen to be here, the prereads, the other topics) or what's going to happen next. They have to talk, listen, absorb, and think.

To manage these collisions, just stay out of their way, remind them how much time they have every now and then, enforce a role if someone strays outside of it, and capture what they're saying to each other.

Here are some examples of memorable collisions. Keep in mind that each example describes *a single collision amongst thousands* that happen every time we run the Formula. And remember too, the megabrain has access to every one of those collisions.

Pablo

Pablo is the CEO of Doregan, a multinational consumer product goods company. It is a large, 40-year-old company that is struggling to be relevant amidst changing consumer preferences and buying habits.

After the agenda-setting exercise, the 36 participants from Doregan and its wider network received a schedule. The schedule outlined the sequence in which the 12 topics would be discussed over the next two and a half days. Each topic had a team assigned to it, with the names of all the members in the group.

Pablo turned to us, looking confused, "I thought I would be in all the teams? Why am I only in a handful of them?"

We responded, assuring him, "You will have access to every team because they're all deliberately connected directly to each other through people's team assignments. Whatever anyone says, whether you hear it firsthand or not, will be fully integrated across the network."

Then the bell rang and everyone headed toward the rooms for their first meetings. There were two teams going on at the same time, each meeting for a little under an hour before taking a break and then moving to the next group. In each room, everyone was held to a disciplined schedule, moving from one room to another like clockwork.

Pablo was getting frustrated as time went on. He kept hearing that he and the executive team were not truly committed to transforming the company into a more customer-centric and digital business. During one meeting, a junior analyst said, "I just get the sense that our leadership team is ignoring the elephant in the room, which is that we've lost touch with our customers and that new customers just don't care nearly as much."

Pablo responded, "You know the leadership team and I discuss this very issue on a weekly basis?"

"Oh," the analyst responded, "I didn't know, but why isn't that urgency communicated to us?"

Then in another meeting, someone made an offhand comment about how the executive team was so focused on meeting quarterly expectations, and thus wouldn't be able to make any real changes. In yet another meeting, one person brought up to the group something he had heard in a different group. Apparently, some people felt that the town hall in which Pablo outlined Doregan's new manifesto was "too abstract and lofty" and that people didn't quite believe it was sincere. Pablo assured the people in that group that he was committed to real, tangible action, but he could tell from people's reactions that the message wasn't getting through.

Finally, he stood up and asserted in a clearly raised voice, "I SWEAR THAT I AM COMMITTED TO THIS," raising one hand in the gesture of taking an oath. Then, with eyes still blazing, he asked, "Do you believe me now?"

That was a key moment for the group. It signaled to everyone that Pablo wasn't just convening everyone in order to go through the motions, and that he wanted serious change. It also signaled to Pablo that while he thought he was being clear in communicating his message of change, it lacked credibility to some who wanted to see real action, commitment, and even pain, and who weren't content with inspirational rhetoric. All of this happened because the megabrain was continuously transmitting signals to Pablo, from many other collision points, that the perception—even after several meetings—continued to be that he and his team were not onboard.

Alicia

Alicia is mental health director at Micbern, a large health system in the Southwest with a network of healthcare facilities and affiliated universities. It is working to mobilize organizations and institutions throughout the state to tackle the mental health crisis.

Alicia was sitting in a room around a table with several others to discuss the topic of optimizing treatment. After five minutes of discussing how emergency room healthcare providers should respond to mentally ill patients in crisis, a psych ER nurse raised the question, "We're so focused on what happens in the emergency room, but we're often not the first responders. The police are. Remember Raymond's story?"

Someone responded, "Yes, I was just thinking about that. If it weren't for the third police officer, the one with experience, coming in, who knows what would've happened to Raymond."

"Well," a law enforcement official in the group interjected, "our force isn't quite trained to be social workers and mental health professionals. That's not what most of our guys signed up for. We became police to maintain law and order, and if someone is acting violently, we don't ask why at first; our priority is to get the situation under control. And at the end of the day, we're accountable for different metrics."

A representative from the state's Department of Health and Human Services responded, "Actually the governor's wife has been convening meetings between our department and the heads of law enforcement this past year, and we would be open to a conversation about new metrics. We think the problem, though, would be training—psychiatric departments are so overworked that we've been assuming they wouldn't be interested or have time to train police officers, especially since we have a very small budget."

The CEO of Micbern stepped in to say, "Budget shouldn't be a concern, not when the stakes are this high. I'd love to offer up our classes and training programs to the wider community; I just never thought law enforcement would be interested. It would be good for us too, to be honest, as it may help us regain some of the trust that I feel people have lost in hospitals, especially with all the news stories of doctors overprescribing to patients."

Alicia found us later and told us about this critical conversation. "You don't understand," she said. "What they talked about and the consensus they came to would've taken months to develop ordinarily. There were so many assumptions made but we were able to cut through all of that so quickly because we got everyone in the room all at once."

CHAPTER 11

Step 8. Advance Iteratively and Emergently

SEBASTIAN THRUN, a Stanford artificial intelligence professor and cofounder of Udacity, said: "Few ideas work on the first try. Iteration is key to innovation."[2]

When you're struggling with complexity, you need to believe that the answers can't be known in advance and thus embrace "emergence" as

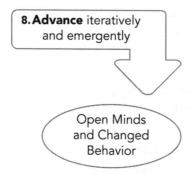

Figure 11-1   Step 8

the vehicle of solving. Your requisite variety group needs to operate with energy and an expectation that the right answers will arise from the right kinds of interactions together.

You don't start with emergence in your requisite variety group; rather, you wait for it once you've created the conditions for the right things to emerge: get the right people together face-to-face, give them the right question and straightforward inputs, ask them what they need to talk about, engineer their collisions, and then let them get to work on answering the question.

Creating those conditions is formulaic, and *iteration* is necessary to supercharge those conditions. Repetition gives the exponential lift to the group; it turns a bunch of individual brains into a functioning megabrain.

Groups don't gel in one step. People don't yield to each other's views in one step. They don't open up to new possibilities, shuck history, arrive at new insights, and reach breakthroughs in one step. Edison didn't invent the lightbulb on the first try. And your requisite variety group with all the right agenda items and an optimally connected network won't resolve their complexity in one go. They can't. As you'll discover, iteration is your ally as you move through your complex challenge. Repetition starts shining a light on the best path forward.

Iteration, Iteration, Iteration

Emergent breakthroughs, insights, answers, clarity, (and so on) require iteration. Having set their agenda, your group needs to go through that entire agenda once, then again, then again. When they do, you'll realize the following benefits:

- Data, information, and knowledge surface; then sharing occurs, not just in one room but across the network;
- People have time to absorb that data, information, and knowledge; reach a shared understanding about what it means; and then share with everyone else that new understanding;

- All participants, in their own time, move off their personal agendas; suspend their opinions; take off their functional, hierarchical, business unit (and so on) hats; set aside their biases; and question their assumptions;

- Data, information, knowledge, and shared understanding "prime the pump" for revisiting each topic, enriched by every topic;

- Iterative cycles on the agenda through your $n(n\text{-}1)$ connected network result in integration, convergence, and emergence.

Iterations work best when you adopt these practices:

- Break them across days to give people unstructured meal time, down time, and sleep time between repetitions;

- Provide guidance on the focus for each iteration. Start with storytelling and information sharing, progress to ideas, and then through to conclusions in successive iterations.

How many iterations? You're probably expecting us to say, "It depends." Interestingly, it doesn't depend. The math says three iterations is ideal—just enough, and one more iteration would yield diminishing returns.

Based on work done to investigate the rate of information diffusion in a connected large-group network space at a session that uses the Formula, 55 percent of the information that must be shared is shared after one iteration; 80 percent is shared after two iterations; and 90 percent is shared after three iterations.

The Secret of Breakthrough Thinking

In *The Eureka Effect: The Art and Logic of Breakthrough Thinking*, David Perkins describes breakthrough thinking as an art and a craft that can be systematized somewhat to bring out its basic patterns and strategies.[3]

Symptom	Response
Overwhelmed	Roving far and wide: "moving around widely in the space of possibilities, looking here, looking there, not lingering long in any one place..."
Clueless	Detecting hidden clues: "although there do not appear to be clues, perhaps there are, if only one looks in a different place..."
Confined	Reframing the situation: "investigate how tacit assumptions, descriptions of the situation, and other factors are constraining the search..."
Beguiled	Decentering from false promise: "backing up to an earlier point and taking a different path from there..."

Figure 11-2   System Response

He then highlights four symptoms felt when in the midst of looking for a breakthrough and names four Logic Operations, or responses to those symptoms:

- When you (or the group) are overwhelmed, *Roving* is the right response;
- When absent the right clues, do some *Detecting*;
- When seemingly confined to a search area that's not bearing fruit, try *Reframing*; and
- When completely beguiled by a solution that seems close but isn't working, it's time for *De-centering.*

We're sharing Perkins' work because it illustrates the value of iterating. You can't "look here and there"; "look in a different place"; negate "tacit assumptions, descriptions of the situation, and other factors"; and "back up from an earlier point and try a different path" in one step.

Now imagine trying to do those things in a large group, in one step.

What Does Emergence Look Like?

An Analogy

If you've ever successfully experienced a Magic Eye book or poster containing autostereograms (which allow some people to see 3-D images by focusing on 2-D patterns) then you know the feeling of having to relax your eyes, suspend your brain's interpretation of what you're looking at, and then notice and refocus on an emergent image suddenly. You can use that experience as a comparison for the emergence we're talking about through the Complexity Formula.

The complexity is the two-dimensional image; the clarity you find is the three-dimensional image that emerges once you are looking for it in the right way. Try this one.

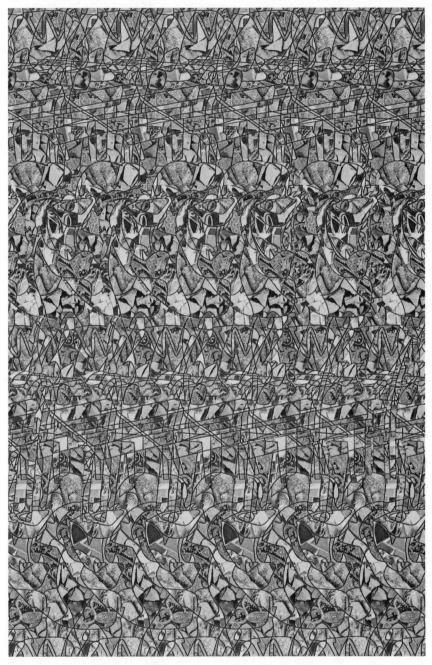

Figure 11-3   Lion Autostereogram

Think of the assembled group, staring at the confounding picture in front of them. Trying to make sense of it. Collectively altering how they focus on finding answers. And suddenly experiencing a moment where an image begins to emerge, then suddenly snaps into place with startling clarity. Not because someone told them what to see but because they looked for it in the right way.

For those who had trouble seeing the three-dimensional "emergent" image, here it is:

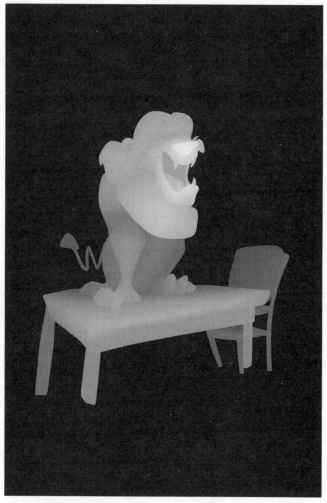

Figure 11-4   Autostereogram Revealed

Three Kinds of Emergence

The sudden recognition of a 3-D image in an autostereogram can give you the sense of wonder, but emergence can take other forms, including:

- *Emergence of clarity* on what's going on within the complex challenge (the various moving parts, the previously hidden interconnections between things) and on the way forward, where previously nothing was clear;

- *Emergence of will*, and ownership, and momentum, and traction, and commitment from everyone in the group on what it will take to successfully execute the solution, where previously progress seemed impossible;

- *Emergence of trust* and empathy among the individuals in the convened group, where previously people didn't know each other, spoke different languages, and had separate, divergent agendas.

All three are critical. All three reflect a state change for the group that can't be arrived at in a linear way, can't be created by someone else for the group, and can't be forced on the group.

Remember the DIKW model (data, information, knowledge, wisdom) from a few chapters ago?

When Ackoff talks about an ounce of knowledge being worth a pound of information, and an ounce of understanding being worth a pound of knowledge, and an ounce of wisdom being worth a pound of understanding, he's expressing layers of emergence: knowledge emerging out of data and information, understanding emerging out of knowledge, and ultimately wisdom emerging out of understanding.

Now let us take you back to our serious and not-so-serious contrasting complicated/complex examples from Chapter 1 so we can use them to further characterize what we mean by emergence:

Complicated/Complex Examples	Not Emergent	Emergent
Having a wedding is complicated; **having a happy marriage is complex**.	A menu for the reception, a selection of flowers	Friendship, love, trust
Fixing a car is complicated; **disrupting the automotive industry is complex**.	Filling the radiator, tightening a lug nut	Market acceptance, driver preferences, competitor response
Placing a bet on a horse race is simple; placing an informed bet is complicated; **the race itself is complex** (if it weren't, you'd only place winning bets).	The field, the favorites, the conditions	The jostling in the paddock, how each horse reacts to the conditions, accidents
Completing a paint-by-numbers image of a landscape is simple; **painting a landscape on a blank canvas is complex**.	Successfully painting each numbered space with the right color	Beauty, color blends, mistakes
Buying a house is complicated; **being a good neighbor is complex**.	Making an offer, paying land transfer tax	Cordiality, respect, disputes and how they're handled
Doing a math assignment is complicated; **doing a writing assignment is complex**.	Successfully applying a formula, showing your work	Creativity, believability, voice, mood

Complicated/Complex Examples	Not Emergent	Emergent
Solving the Rubik's cube is complicated—maybe even simple; **establishing this product as a world-wide sensation and commercial success was complex**.	Speed of applying the steps and reaching a solution	Fads, viral uptake, word of mouth
Building a rocket that can put a person on the moon is merely complicated; **rallying the country to create the conditions where it could happen fast, that was complex**.	Engineering, simulations, a splash landing	The impact of a charismatic and visionary leader, the public's response to fear of a Cold War enemy
Implementing a customer relationship management system is complicated; **delivering a winning customer experience consistently is complex**.	User requirements, successful installation of software and hardware, bug-tracking systems and processes	Customer satisfaction, trust, relationship
Installing a new enterprise-wide accounting system is complicated; **taking 10 points out of SG&A without harming the business is complex**.	Business process and policy changes, new instructions on how to submit expenses	Impact on work-life balance, incentives, customer experience with finance-related processes

Complicated/Complex Examples	Not Emergent	Emergent
Rolling out idea management software is complicated; **creating and executing on a robust innovation agenda is complex**.	Submitting ideas and voting on others' ideas	Culture of innovation, breakthrough ideas, resonance of ideas
Implementing an ERP system to enable transformation is complicated; **transforming is complex**.	Process change, new bar-code scanners	Mind-set, behavior, employee satisfaction, successful leadership

Iteration through the connected collisions on the chosen topics creates emergence. Emergence is something you can't force but you can engineer; repetition is a must.

As one participant, a scientist, described his experience after the third round of meetings on all topics: "I can't put my finger exactly on what or how, but something *magic* just happened here." That "magic" is the feeling of sudden convergence and emergence of clarity and solution along with ownership and commitment, alignment and belief, mobilization, and will that you can expect when you trust the Complexity Formula to deliver the goods. We'll get into the rest of the conditions necessary to create that magic in the next chapter.

How to Advance Iteratively and Emergently

To allow for emergence, and information flow, and behavior change, and shared understanding, and thinking and deciding, and, and, and . . . you need iteration. Not one kick at each can, not two, but three. And with all

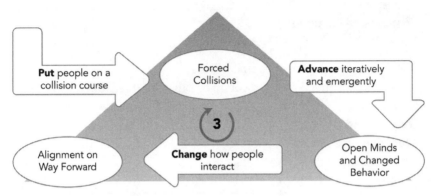

Figure 11-5   10-Step Highlight: Collision

that's going on, all the robust collisions and great people interacting, all the learning and signal detection, all the breakthroughs and insights—you need to be diligently looking for what emerges, not trying to fit what emerges into your preconceived notion of how things are.

Complexity is an entanglement of a whole bunch of facets. The agenda created by your group reflects those facets, each in isolation. Your network structure connects those facets and the conversations about them, and then drives people into collisions with each other in the context of those facets.

One conversation won't cut it. To create the required number of collisions, you need three rounds of conversations on each of those facets—the mathematics and our experience have demonstrated that three times is the charm.

If you recall the illustration of the 10 steps that we started with, you'll see that steps 7, 8, and 9 account for the three rounds of iterating.

Progression and Sequence Across Iterations

Use an "it is," "we could," and "we should" progression to the three iterations.

- The "it is" iteration is a status quo discussion covering all the issues and opportunities, information sharing, and storytelling;

- The "we could" is about idea generation in an unconstrained fashion, deliberately held back from drawing conclusions and making recommendations;
- The "we will" is where specific, action-oriented recommendations are made.

In linear problem solving, sequence is paramount. You can't do step 5, then go back to step 2, then step 1, then step 6. Even if you iterate through the sequence a second time, the broken first sequence means a door can't be attached or a shelf can't be shoved in (to use the assembling-a-bookcase example).

In nonlinear problem solving, which is what we're talking about here, sequence doesn't matter. Even if there is a logical sequence to the complexity's multiple facets, by its very nature that sequence can't be known until after you've figured things out.

We hear it all the time: "Don't we have to talk about our corporate image before talking about what we promise our customers?" or "Shouldn't we talk about who the customer is before talking about driving customer value?" or "How can we talk about how we train our people, when we haven't yet sorted out what capabilities we need to develop?"

In fact, in the complex domain these various facets have multiple interconnections and overlaps, and you can easily talk yourself into or out of any sequence being the right sequence. To use the first example above, "Don't we have to talk about our corporate image before talking about what we promise customers?" could easily be turned around as "Shouldn't our corporate image reflect what we can promise our customers?"

The actual sequence of topics doesn't matter. What matters is keeping that sequence intact in all three iterations. The systematic repetition ensures optimal and balanced information flow and stepwise progress across topics toward macro answers.

When you follow the pattern "it is," "we could," "we will," it plays out in a predictable way in each iteration.

Expectations for Iteration 1

- Iteration 1 is about getting people to share information and level-set on language without any meaningful progress on answering the question.

- Lots of storytelling and griping. People have a lot to unload and it needs to happen now. People need to complain about how the organization has ignored a start-up for years that has now become a competitive threat; they need to talk about how the environment has changed and tell a story that illustrates the change in dramatic terms. The point is sharing information, so lots of storytelling is great.

- A feeling of no, or backward, progress. It is normal to feel further away from answers than when you started. Collision team meetings end when time is up, as opposed to ending when people reach consensus. Nothing is resolved yet. Solving hasn't happened yet. So it can be frustrating.

Expectations for Iteration 2

- Some good idea generation is happening in some places; in other places people are struggling to think big. Not all teams will be created equal; some will get to storming and performing, while others will be stuck on forming and norming. Let each team move at their own pace. If you try to rescue them, you'll get in the way and remove their accountability to figure things out.

- Some teams may feel "done" after round 2. They're not done because it's not over until you've heard from the last team. Everything may change in iteration 3. That's typical of emergence.

Expectations for Iteration 3

- Extraordinary collision team meetings are the norm: hyperproductive teams, free-flowing and effective conversations, and very solid or fast convergence and consensus on recommendations.

- Most teams that struggled through the first two iterations end up with strong results in iteration 3.

How to Plan and Prepare for Emergence

People like to plan and prepare. If they're doing a presentation, they arrive early and make sure everything is properly set up. If they're planting a garden, they carefully tend the beds and get the soil ready long before dropping in the seeds or saplings. If they're solving a complicated challenge, they look ahead through the instructions to see what tools they're going to need to ensure they have everything.

Attacking a complex challenge isn't like that. Answers *emerge*, they aren't preknown. How do you plan and prepare for that?

We get asked that a lot.

You plan for emergence by expecting it to happen anywhere and at any time. You set up collisions that will drive it to happen, you pay attention to what's happening at the collision points, and then you sit and wait. It's like the autostereograms we showed you as an analogy earlier—focus your eyes the right way, empty your mind, stare and wait. Unforced, a 3-D image will suddenly appear.

Likewise, with all the steps in place that we've been discussing, emergence is going to happen. You'll know you experienced it afterward even if you don't remember when exactly it happened.

Because we run ourselves through the Complexity Formula (on our customer experience, on our account strategy, on improving the draft of this book), we have experienced emergence for ourselves firsthand. Whether it's an insight around how to help our sponsors do a better job of inviting their requisite variety, or clarity on some things to try with our accounts, or a better way of expressing a concept in our book—these things pop when they're ready to. You create the conditions and make yourself ready to detect what's emerging.

That's how you plan. That's how you prepare. All of the steps before this one, including the iteration called for in this step, *are* the planning and preparing steps for emergence.

When Einstein talks about groping, his sage advice is predicated on personal experience with emergence. He didn't know in advance what was going to emerge, but he did know that when he did the right things to create the right conditions, *something* would.

Great stand-up comics are like that too. They deliver their best lines when they go off-script, when they interact with audience members, or when something happens they weren't planning for. They don't know what's going to happen or how they're going to respond, but they trust their ability to find the right words in the right moment. The comedy emerges from what's going on around them, and they're just attuned to everything, waiting for the right moment.

Pablo

> Pablo is the CEO of Doregan, a multinational consumer product goods company. It is a large, 40-year-old company that is struggling to be relevant amidst changing consumer preferences and buying habits.

By the end of the first of three days together, Pablo noticed that most people around him were feeling frustrated and impatient.

"We've surfaced a lot of important things but it's all a mess, and I have no clue how we're going to come up with solutions in just two more days," one person said to him when Pablo asked him how it was going.

Another said, "We spent so much time today sharing information; it's just learning and learning, which is good, but we haven't even really come to a consensus on what the problem is that we are trying to solve."

When Pablo told us this, we responded that this is what happens on the first day. When you have such a diverse array of participants, it's natural that the first day is primarily about information sharing, defining scope, and getting it all out on the table so that people can eventually start speaking the same language, even if they haven't yet used that language to build answers.

Pablo nodded but added, "I get that, and I trust you. My main concern is that people are still pretty deferential to me when I'm in the room. I do get challenged but often in a casual, offhand way or under the breath when they don't think I can hear."

When we pressed him for an example, he told us about the last meeting he was in.

Pablo decided to toss out what he thought was a fairly provocative statement: "What if Doregan invested in our own e-commerce platform?"

The room was silent for a second and then most people started nodding at the idea. A few even threw in other ideas for how to differentiate the platform from other prominent online players.

Then Pablo switched tracks and said, "But that would mean starting an entirely different business within our company, and it's probably not worth the effort." The same people who were nodding five minutes ago were nodding yet again.

"Yeah, it's probably not worth it," they said.

Pablo narrated this incident to us in frustration. "It definitely felt like people were tiptoeing around me. I'd challenge, I'd question, I'd make statements I wasn't sure I believed, and people just looked the other way, held their tongues, and nodded. And as a CEO, I want honesty. That's the only way we can make progress."

"Wait till you all meet again on that topic for the second time," we told him. "Then tell us if you're observing the same thing."

By the time the second iteration rolled around, he noticed a change. He started to regularly get challenged by the people in the room. When he tried to aggressively dismiss a suggestion without letting the person finish, he was interrupted and the person who was dismissed was asked to finish his idea. When Pablo replied, "Oh, we can't do that," to an idea about pop-up stores and incorporating memes in their digital advertising, people pushed him to defend his position and explain why.

An important moment occurred when a midlevel communications director in the team discussing "next-gen customers" interrupted Pablo midsentence and said, "Pablo, you keep talking about how millennials are relating to shopping and consumer goods differently. I think we're missing the bigger point: It's not about engaging millennials, it's about adapting to a changing consumer base, which affects everything from our products to our supply chain to our workplace culture and diversity, not to mention our marketing. If not, as stable and historied as our brand is, if things continue, the only chance my great-grandkids will know about what I do now is in the hallways of museums."

That statement synthesized various strands and streams of thought that had been emerging in the past two iterations from various teams. It marked a turning point for that specific group—after that, they started to change who they defined as the "emerging customer"—but also for all the groups. The phrase "the hallways of museums" started reverberating through other groups, waking up a lot of people, especially longtime employees, to what was at stake for Doregan.

Best of all for Pablo, the iteration sparked an emergent behavior that he had been trying to encourage in his people for years: speaking honestly and openly with each other, and parking hierarchy at the door when it came to resolving important issues for the customer.

Brenda

Brenda is SVP of finance at Plesius Finacorp, a financial services company, which has a 10-year-old partnership with Danley-Ross HealthAge, a seniors association. The partnership has been vastly underperforming compared to its potential.

"How is everything going?" we asked Brenda during the lunch break on the second day. All groups had already met twice, and they would meet for the third and final round later in the afternoon.

"I feel like some concrete action plans are emerging," she said. "We're still sharing and learning new information, but now the conversation is more focused on solving."

"But," she said, "I don't know if I'm seeing any really bold and captivating ideas that are really exciting people's passion. In some ways this is typical for us."

Brenda went to her topic groups for the third round and decided to try and kick things up a notch.

"I remember earlier in my career at my old consulting firm," she began the discussion, "I had a new boss who came in and rallied her team around a simple, focused, and aggressive rallying cry, 'We were going to *annihilate* the competition.'"

"Now, in this case, it's a partnership and not the competition," she continued, "but I think we need that level of fervor and urgency—dare I say, aggression—in approaching this opportunity. Danley-Ross' members ought to receive financial advice and planning as early as possible—the longer we wait, the longer we do them a disservice."

After that comment, the room started buzzing with both excitement and anxiety around how to raise the level of urgency. The rallying cry "Beat the clock" was developed in that meeting, and members of that group carried that catchphrase to their other meetings.

Every other team that subsequently met stepped up and applied a much stronger tone and stance in their own recommendations. The emergent tone took root in a small group meeting and then spread to the rest of the group. The 500 percent target now seemed very realistic; people started throwing around ideas about how to go even higher. Eventually, the group started hitting upon some breakthrough, out-of-the-box ideas and action plans (more on that in the next chapter).

Sometimes it takes the third time through the agenda topics for a new truth to emerge for everyone and for people to realize they need to take a different path in solving. The connected network and repeated collisions mean that when this happens in one room, it naturally and immediately spreads to all the other topics so they can readjust accordingly.

CHAPTER **12**

Step 9. Change How People Interact

W HEN WE TALKED EARLIER about engineering serendipity through forced collisions, we were focused on $n(n\text{-}1)$ connectivity and how that brings all the right people in contact with each other multiple times to produce opportunities for "magic."

The collisions and a co-created agenda give context for serendipity to happen, but there's more to it than that. You also have to create the right conditions at each collision point to bring about formulaic "magic," or as C. Otto Scharmer would call it, "alchemy":

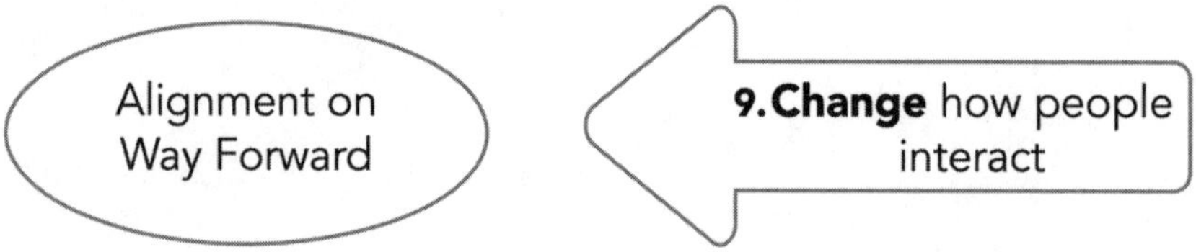

Figure 12-1   Step 9

It's hard work. And you cannot engineer it in the old way, which is by controlling it. But you can create conditions that allow a deeper alchemy to work—that is, conditions that help leaders in a system to broaden and deepen their view of the system from ego to eco, from 'me' to 'we.'[1]

When we earlier mentioned the scientist/participant who remarked on his feeling that "something magic" had happened after having been through the Complexity Formula, that's the sense of alchemy we mean here: "A seemingly magical process of transformation, creation, or combination." But only "seemingly magical," because it's a step-by-step Formula.

What are the conditions that drive that alchemy?

Iterating toward Ideal Conditions

From our experience, remarkable outcomes result, and not by accident, when collision teams are brought together on any given topic and the following conditions exist:

- The group is sitting down to achieve a clear and ambitious task with a brief amount of time to do so. Strict time discipline has become the norm for the group.
- Everybody needed to achieve that task is in the room, and nobody extra is there.
- Everybody is comfortable with everybody else around the table. They have come to understand each other's positions, opinions, and perspectives, and they've heard each other's stories. They are listening well to each other, contributing equally, and have developed a high degree of trust.
- They have clear and well-understood roles to play in their discussion.

- They have shared everything they need to share and learned each other's language, and now the pump is well primed with all the necessary signals filtered out from the noise.

- Since they last met as a collision team, everyone around their table has spoken to many other people on other collision teams who have a stake in their discussion. Through those interactions, they are all up to speed on what is happening with a bunch of other teams who have been iterating on connected and highly relevant topics.

- They have access to an accurate, real-time record of their prior conversations, and all of the other conversations that are relevant.

- They all understand what is at stake and jointly feel accountable for results.

Changing How People Interact

As collision teams interact, what happens that creates alchemy? What makes the conditions ideal? This is where the rubber hits the road in terms of the massive opportunity you've engineered.

Acceleration and progress are already enabled by the right people, iteration, connectedness, and so on. But despite all those other characteristics, the group will slow down and even stop if their interactions are unproductive.

This step is all about making sure human interactions are effective: candid, incisive, unconstrained, unguarded, transparent, fierce, and focused.

That requires:

- Discipline and structure
- Right-sized teams
- Effective conversation roles
- An environment where productive friction is expected, not frowned upon
- Neutral tour guide/note-taker

Don't be fooled by how mundane these requirements may seem. They lead to faster, more effective, more direct, and more genuine conversations. Without ensuring these things, the eight prior steps can easily set-up accelerated but same-old-same-old discussions.

Discipline and Structure

Teams become productive when they are operating in a "container" with clear goals, rules, and time frames that are fair (i.e., everyone has to follow them) and reasonable. With all of the complexity involved in human dynamics, reducing some of that variety without stifling creativity or freedom paves the way for much faster progress.

For example, you're not going to get anywhere without clarity on what you're trying to do. You won't feel any pressure if you don't have a time limit. You risk spinning your wheels in one place if you're not occasionally doing a "process check" on where you are and whether you're doing the right things.

Here we're talking about the discipline and structure provided by the container: A schedule, a clock, overarching discussion principles, and goals.

Time discipline and time pressure are enormously powerful forces that few take seriously. When you've engineered the right conditions, groups experience accelerated performance as a result of effective use of time pressure.

Right-sized Teams

Collision teams, consisting of no more than eight people, can have productive interactions. With more than eight participants, conversations are dominated by a few and tuned out by the rest. When there's not enough talk time to go around, people choose one or the other behavior: talk more and don't share the floor or disengage and do something else without being noticed.

Effective Conversation Roles

As people have formal interactions, they benefit from specific guidance on how they're expected to participate and the purpose of their participation.

Simple and clear roles make all of this clear for each person. These roles need to be equally assigned and enforced, but that doesn't preclude people playing different roles at different times in different interactions, as long as it all adds up equally across all of the interactions.

We use roles that deliberately challenge, question, and provide tension within interactions. We also use them to divide up talk time so that even if there are more than an optimal number of people in the room, those who can speak at a given time are collision-team size. These roles break people's usual way of interacting—not listening, taking notes, making speeches, loudest voices dominating, hierarchy dominating, and so forth. We use Stafford Beer's member, critic, and observer roles to eliminate these patterns, giving everyone an equal chance to play each one:

Members

Members are at the table and are accountable for results. They own the conversation and they ultimately drive to conclusions. They do the bulk of the talking. They are a subset of requisite variety, and they'll have a good mix of perspectives *and* interest in the topic they're discussing.

Critics

Critics sit back from members, listen to their conversation, and intermittently get the floor to offer their critique. They might tell them "you're being too polite," or "you're diving into detail too soon," or "one of my previous collision teams just landed on something that contradicts what you just concluded," or anything else that will help the members have a better outcome. There is no back-and-forth between members and critics.

Observers

Observers listen and aren't allowed to talk at all during the course of the conversation. For some, this is a tremendously refreshing and highly valuable role. For others, it's torture. Whether valuable or torturous, because the roles are assigned equally, observers are also members and critics on other topics. While this role is passive from a conversational standpoint, it's cognitively active. Observers have a chance to think deeply and reflect on the conversations, which enriches their contributions in the other two roles they will play in other conversations.

As you divide people into these roles, you grant discussion rights to them role by role. When members are talking to each other, no one else can. When critics are offering feedback, everyone listens. Observers don't get to speak at all while this topic is happening. For this reason, members are effectively a collision team, as are critics and observers. All three collision teams are interacting with each other (sometimes listening, sometimes speaking amongst themselves), so these roles enable you to put more people into each topic and to engineer more collisions amongst them, while keeping those collisions effective.

An Environment Where Conflict and Tension are Expected, Not Frowned Upon

When you're dealing with complex challenges, no amount of avoidance is going to make conversations easy, straightforward, or harmonious. The natural tensions in the system, the conflict, the issues, the worries, the barriers—they're all important aspects of the complexity. They need to be dealt with and overcome to get to the other side.

Good interactions don't just make it safe for people to be frank and honest (while being respectful); they demand it. They are designed to bring those messy and potentially uncomfortable discussions to the forefront, because if they aren't dealt with while all the right people are together, they won't be dealt with at all.

People have to speak their mind forcefully and fearlessly given the outcomes you're driving for. Note that we're not saying a "safe environment"—although that's part of it, in terms of there being no repercussions for the behavior you're asking people to display (frankness, critical thinking, genuine opinion, challenging each other, etc.).

The senior-most person there should say, "It's okay to say anything," but needs to go further than that: "What's not okay is to say something two weeks from now that you held back from saying here." Then—that senior-most person and everyone else with any kind of positional or power advantage—needs to walk the talk. It often helps more junior people to see the senior people challenging each other before they'll be convinced that it's okay to do so.

Very importantly, the permission to challenge, the provocation to be frank, the invitation to check hierarchy at the door—all of that has to be genuine. Savvy organizational old-timers can smell a trap a mile away.

The member, critic, and observer roles also help people to "bring it" because those roles (particularly the critic) force people to speak, to listen, and to challenge each other in ways they don't normally do.

Neutral Tour Guide/Note-Taker

The group needs someone in the room with them, holding them to time discipline and conversation roles. But they don't need what you would traditionally term a "facilitator" because that often also includes an expectation of involvement, content contribution, personality, and even discussion leadership that we don't mean here.

The group needs a tour guide/note-taker, someone who isn't talking or drawing attention to themselves, but is:

- Looking at the clock
- Listening to the group
- Coordinating the roles
- Providing the occasional reminder
- Taking great notes

Find someone who can be completely neutral in their management of the conversations and their capture of what happens in the collision teams.

Make sure that in their notes, they remain unbiased and accurate, and that they don't worry about who said what. If you weren't in the room, the notes must give you a great sense of the conversation and the consensus reached, and no idea who said what.

Interactions in Traditional Meetings

Nobody wants bad interactions; it's just that they're the norm when you talk about traditional meetings.

Many of the problems with traditional meetings go away when they are short and involve the right number of people. If you believe in adequate variety, however, a small number of people isn't adequate for complex challenges. You're usually looking at 24-plus people. Traditional meeting formats produce bad interactions and bad results with large groups.

If you think about the many methodologies and processes out there that are used to deal with a range of complex tasks—from business process improvement to innovation to strategic planning to stakeholder engagement—most require the involvement of lots of people and occasional times where many of those people are brought together (or should be) for large group meetings. These are the make-or-break moments for many methods and processes (whether Lean, Design Thinking, or Agile).

The "magic" of good interactions isn't magic at all, but it does require careful attention to detail so that the conditions exist where preparation can meet opportunity.

Brenda

> Brenda is SVP of finance at Plesius Finacorp, a financial services company, which has a 10-year-old partnership with Danley-Ross HealthAge, a seniors association. The partnership has been vastly underperforming compared to its potential.

It took some time for Thad Holmes to warm up to his first topic group. The topic was Understanding Danley-Ross' Members' Financial Needs, and Holmes found himself unable to talk. He was assigned the role of "observer," where he simply had to listen; he couldn't say a word during the meeting. We were observers in the same topic group, and we noticed that he was preoccupied with responding to emails on his phone. Then someone in the room said something that caught his attention. She said:

"We've got to stop thinking of our members as out-of-touch. Grandparents are on social media. How else do they stay in touch with updates on their grandkids? Forty percent of seniors age 65 or older are smartphone owners.[2] So of course online reviews of our financial products and services are important."

Holmes wanted to argue back and say, "That doesn't sound like the grandparents I know," but he couldn't. The conversation intrigued him, however: 40 percent was a higher statistic than he ever would have guessed.

In his next topic, Marketing On-Brand, his group was discussing how to expand outreach to Danley-Ross' members while staying within the parameters of Danley-Ross' brand and ethos. Holmes felt many of the ideas that were being proposed went against how he believed Living Well should act toward its community.

"Especially after recent news of elder fraud, seniors are wary about where they invest their money. We don't want to sound like we are promoting schemes," he said.

Plesius' VP of client services, annoyed by Holmes' insinuation, replied tersely, "Our senior specialists are top-of-line. They know our clients inside out, and building trust with them is our top priority. That's why we're so well regarded in our industry."

"And we will convey that to our members in person or over the phone, I'm just not convinced it can take place through mobile, digital ads, as seniors aren't likely to trust that as reliable sources of information," a member coordinator at Danley-Ross replied.

Brenda piped up, "But the only way we can hit 500 percent growth is if we invest in mobile and digital; there's no way around it."

"Hang on," Holmes said, taking off his glasses. "In the other meeting, someone said something about how four in 10 seniors own smartphones and more than a third use social networking sites. We may need to start taking social or mobile marketing more seriously."

Everyone paused, shocked that Holmes was talking about the increasing importance of mobile marketing to seniors.

The scribe, who was taking notes this whole time, broke the silence to say, "It's time for critics to speak."

One of the critics, a social media director at Plesius, said, "You all are having the same version of the arguments again and again. It seems like many of you operate from the same assumptions about what mobile advertising could look like. Isn't there an advertising consultant in your group? I'd like to hear more from her."

After the critics were done, Holmes turned to the advertising consultant, Kyu Oh, to his right. "You're the ad person, right?" Holmes asked. "What are we missing or getting wrong?"

"Well," Kyu coughed before responding, "I think I tried to say this before but perhaps I wasn't clear. There are many ways to market yourself beyond ads. You can create sponsored content that's in line with your brand . . . "

The conversation went on in that group for two more rounds before the final round.

"Okay everyone, this is your final round. You have to produce three concrete recommendations to bring before the entire group," the scribe explained. "So start thinking in terms of concrete things you can do and things you can try."

Ten minutes into the meeting, Sasha decided to throw onto the table an idea she'd been developing: "We've been talking about how we need to 'beat the clock.' And that means getting to our members while they're still in their 50s, right? Well, one opportunity exists because of their relative youth: At that age, they likely still have at least one living parent in their 70s or 80s."

"So . . . ?"Brenda replied, puzzled.

She took in a breath and continued, "Why not target those younger members with a financial planning offering that helps them talk with their parents and understand their parents' financial situations and needs? I know many people struggle with that and would see the help and advice as much needed. Our younger members are the most likely to be active on social media . . . so it makes perfect sense to offer them a service that is so personally important in the same places where they're sharing photos and stories about what's going on in their lives. And what's more, they will become aware of the program being available for their own financial planning as well . . . but not in a way that makes them feel like targets."

She explained how this idea touched on many of the themes they had discussed across several topics, including activating younger members as advocates of the program, and increasing awareness with unaffiliated seniors—in this case, the parents of members. It was a bold idea, and everyone in the room looked at Holmes for his reaction. He was the de facto gatekeeper of the "community" and protector of the brand.

"I like it," he said, after a pause.

"Really, you do?" Sasha asked, the look of surprise evident on her face.

"Yes, I think it solves a few of the problems we've been circling around for the past day and a half, and it's got a very personal feel to it that's a great fit with our brand. I don't think anyone would be offended by it."

Sasha's idea to create a new campaign directed at younger members and their need to talk about finances with their parents ended up being the most popular recommendation from the entire group.

After the session ended, Holmes turned to us to tell us about his experience.

"You have no idea," he said, eyes large with excitement, "when I first got here, I was on my phone for the first few exercises. I didn't care."

"But then once we got into small groups, that was when I was really forced outside of my comfort zone. I'm a big extrovert and verbal processor—debater, some would say—and to be forced just to listen was hard."

He explained to us how he was feeling during the first topic group, but also how he brought in the ideas he absorbed from that group into his second topic group, Marketing On-Brand.

"I think all of those bits and pieces finally added up to Sasha's idea in the third and final round," he said. "Then everything fell into place."

After he left the room, Sasha came up to us and said, "Just so you know, that may have been the first time that Holmes has ever reacted positively to a big idea I've had. I've come up with similar ideas before—the only difference was that today, he was listening."

CHAPTER 13

Step 10. Translate Clarity and Insights into Action

A NOTHER WAY TO THINK about the impact of your complex challenge—why you can't easily see your way forward, why you need clarity—is to characterize it as a heavy mist obscuring your vision (as in Stephen King's *The Mist* but without the monsters). Progress requires you to penetrate the mist.

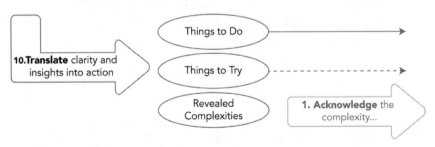

Figure 13-1   Step 10

As you wade into it, you're always going to see what's in your immediate surroundings and nothing more. You shuffle forward a bit, see if you're about to walk into a building or trip over a curb, and adjust accordingly. That's what Tom Peters, a business management writer, meant in his article "The Best Corporate Strategy? None of Course" when he wrote, "Life is pretty simple: You do some stuff. Most fails. Some works. You do more of what works."[1] You can't penetrate the mist without a trial-and-error approach.

When you apply the steps we've been taking you through, you've analogously pulled together and connected with a team of all the right people to navigate the mist together. As a result of the size of the group and its connectedness, you've got a wider field of vision, greater clarity on the immediate surroundings, and the ability to move forward much faster and with more confidence.

Three Categories of Action

The actions that result from the use of the Complexity Formula fall into three categories: things to do, things to try, and newly revealed complexities. Moving forward means gaining clarity and shared understanding on how to execute on all three categories:

- *Simple and complicated* (well-known, well-understood) *next steps.* These are *things to do*, and you should just do them.

- *Experiments* (pilots, prototypes, tests) to conduct. These are *things to try*, and you should just try them so that you either fail fast or succeed fast and learn accordingly.

- *Newly revealed complexities* that next need to be addressed. These new complexities require a new question, new requisite variety, and so on.

For Doregan, the Complexity Formula produced (for example):

- A few quick wins like:
  - Changes they needed to make to their back-office systems to capture more customer information, and the staff training they needed to create and deliver as a result.

- Some website and packaging enhancements they needed to make so that Doregan's values were better reflected.

- Some procedural work they needed to do so that costs and risks within supply chain were better managed.

- Accelerated green lights on two divestitures and one acquisition, and the launch of a new, clearly focused innovation platform. These are all examples of things to do.

- Some great ideas around current products and how to set up a prototype in one or two major cities to quickly find out what buyers thought of the products. They also came away with ideas about how to make it easier to peruse and buy their products through e-commerce platforms and even Instagram. They wanted to start with undergraduate students, and they came up with a list of local campuses they should use for those pilots. These are examples of things to try.

- New complexities that required "drill-down" recursion of the Complexity Formula, including a recommended "big data" play and an enterprise-wide talent strategy.

How to Translate Clarity and Insights into Action

Having reached the point with the Complexity Formula where clarity and insights have emerged, step 10 is about separating the work into the three piles listed above and attacking each pile in the right way to make progress, to continue learning, and to get after the next big challenge.

For example, consider a requisite variety group that's been brought together to figure out how to make a chain of laundromats more user-friendly, relevant, and future-ready. The clarity and insights they find could include statements like:

- People who use laundromats love to read. There's a great opportunity for us to partner with digital players like Amazon and

Goodreads to make e-readers available while people wait for their laundry to dry.

- Some people would be willing to pay for a concierge service. It's only a matter of time before someone brings e-laundry to the market. That should be us.

- Nano-enhanced textiles and clothes that clean themselves will one day put us out of business. We need to be at the forefront of that technology so we can transition into that business when the time comes.

When these and other insights from the laundromat are sorted into the three piles, they'd have:

- *Things to do.* The straightforward tasks identified in answering the question—including finding and cutting a deal with an e-reader/content partner.

- *Things to try.* The pilots, experiments, tests, trials (etc.) that were identified—including experimenting with a small-scale e-laundry concierge service in one of their stores' communities.

- *Emerging complexities.* The new complexities that you couldn't see at first—including the disruptive threat of self-cleaning clothes.

Things to Do

The simple or complicated *things to do* represent straight-line opportunities to make progress (yourself or with outside help).

The common thread is usually that the *things to do* are either part of some function's day job (e.g., finance or IT), or they feed into existing projects (e.g., an ERP implementation that's underway), or they could require new workstreams/projects to make them happen.

But in all three cases, they can easily be budgeted for, assigned time lines, assigned ownership, and launched.

That's not the end of them, nor do you launch them and then look away and trust they'll get done. They need tracking, they need to be managed, they might need to be championed. But it's fairly straightforward to get them going.

Quick Wins

Some of the *things to do* will qualify as "quick wins" in that they can be implemented without waiting for any further decisions to be made or any other work to get done. These are gold if any of them are highly visible or high impact and fast to get done.

Get your quick wins done right away and use them to communicate that you're serious about taking action on what the group told you has to happen.

A good quick win or two will be a highlight in the first communication back to the organization after applying the Complexity Formula.

Things to Try

Usually, the plan also contains a small number of important experiments (which might be referred to as pilots, or prototypes, or test cases) related to an idea that the group was excited about but not yet certain it would work. Or, if they were certain, they might have suggested a pilot as a proof-of-concept to be scaled up later.

The *things to try* require more planning, more oversight, and more discipline than the *things to do*. If it's going to be a legitimate experiment, some time should be spent stating a hypothesis, designing the method, identifying how to measure success and what metrics should be baked in to do so, figuring out who will do the assessment and when they will do it, and deciding on what actions will be taken in various result scenarios.

Executing well on experiments, trials, pilots, and prototypes is often a gap in organizations' internal capabilities. The ability to design and conduct proper experiments is going to become increasingly important for organizations dealing with complexity. You may have to develop and/or flex muscles around setting up, monitoring, and evaluating experiments, and you can also look to partner organizations with experimentation capabilities to design and run these tests with you.

Newly Revealed Complexities

Remember our Second Rule of Q: "When it comes to jumping into complexity, do that from any part of the deck because it's all one pool." Often, jumping in on one complexity naturally reveals others that require resolution.

Until your sports team figures out the complexity of making the play-offs, you can't see how challenging it is going to be to take the next step and win the championship. Until you've taken your organization into the digital age, you can't see the complexities of winning there. Until you've navigated the complexity of successfully acquiring a new business unit, you can't see the nuances and obstacles of integrating the two cultures.

By now, you know what to do with these new complexities. DON'T PRETEND THEY'RE MERELY COMPLICATED. Don't outsource them to a so-called expert. Start up the Complexity Formula again by acknowledging the complexity, defining the next question, selecting the requisite variety group, and getting them together.

What to Do with the Plan

You've established your overall plan and have distinguished among the things to do, things to try, and the newly revealed complexities.

Next, you need to worry about ongoing governance and management of the plan, and communication about it to several audiences.

The Complexity Formula secures precious clarity, shared understanding, buy-in, alignment, and mobilization. Precious, because those qualities weren't there before and they've always been elusive. You've struck a match and the kindling is burning, and now it has to be kept burning, the flame has to grow, and it has to continue to sustainably burn and grow.

Without good governance, the flame can go out. Without great communication, it won't spread (and this—metaphorically—is a flame you want to spread).

The catalyst for the Formula was a complex challenge—and now you've got it cornered and at bay. You know what needs to be done. You know who needs to do what. And you know what everybody in the organization now needs to know: *That* you're going to win and *how* you're going to win. The basic blocking-and-tackling of governance, plan management, and communication are now essential.

Governance

Decide which senior person will own/champion the resulting plan, who the project manager will be, and what core team will steer it.

Set up a light-touch governance process, so the champion, PM, and core team are in regular meetings, tracking progress, being made aware of issues and removing barriers, and keeping an eye on the overall coherence of the plan (are activities and people staying in sync, are interdependencies being taken care of, etc.)

Good project managers or PMOs know how to stay on top of the individual work items, so their job is to keep everyone else informed. The champion and core team are both A) representatives from the requisite variety group that co-created the plan (and can thus stay true to what that group concluded and why), and B) internal influencers and decision makers who can intervene as necessary to keep things moving ahead.

Don't lump this plan in with all of the other "projects" and "initiatives" underway in the organization. Those other efforts are sending people around the organization all the time, asking for interviews and other kinds of contributions, and people become very adept at ducking their heads and waiting for them to go away. Assuming the complexity that the plan is meant to solve is core and strategic, it's not "just another project"; it's a strategic pillar and should be positioned and communicated that way.

Communication

There are several audiences with whom to communicate, and several points in time when that communication is critical. We use the following table with our customers to show them a tried-and-true structure for their communication plan:

Audience	Now	Soon (2 Weeks)	Ongoing
Participants / Requisite Variety Group	Thank you, raw output from the conversations	Report out of results	Regular progress and status updates
Action Owners	Heads up with details to follow	Their actions and the relevant details from the group	Status updates from them and overall plan updates to them
Executives (Board)	Brief summary of output Request for support?	Action plan for approval Expectations of the leadership team	Dashboard
Everyone	Why that illustrious group was away / what they got done	Description of the overall plan	Regular updates on progress

Of particular import, but not well represented in the table above, is the need to "spread the word" (and the optimism, clarity, shared understanding, etc.) out to everyone who wasn't part of the requisite variety group. For example:

- The cynics who weren't there are still cynics;
- The leaders who weren't there don't know what they are going to be asked to lead;
- The action owners (doers) who weren't there don't have full context for what they're supposed to do;
- Everyone else doesn't know what's going on; they don't have any new information and they may still be wallowing in the complexity.

Given that all these key people are outside of the complexity loop, they need to be informed what's taken place. Here are some tactics that work well:

- In presenting the final plan to leadership, have a subset of the requisite variety group attend the meeting and share the stage in describing the plan, then answer questions. What will be enlightening to those who didn't participate in the Formula is how these previously unaligned people can now finish each other's sentences;

- Send out a regular communiqué to the whole organization (status of the plan, progress in addressing the complex challenge). This keeps the effort top-of-mind for people, demonstrates follow-through, and makes it clear this isn't just another project;

- Give participants from the requisite variety group a brief presentation they can use in their individual jurisdictions to tell the story of what they participated in and what is going on as a result. Remember, one of the characteristics you scanned for in choosing the group was their internal and external influence; the influencers in particular are key in spreading the word.

Drill-Downs and Fan-Outs

It is normal and to be expected that clarity in the face of complexity will include things to do, things to try, and newly revealed complexities. When we help organizations implement the Complexity Formula, we tell them as much up front, and we talk about what that means: They will need good old-fashioned project management and project governance to manage the resulting action plan; they will need to be ready to run some experiments and track their progress; and they should be prepared to get after some new complexities.

Sometimes we can even plan in advance with them for drill-down and fan-out programs.

A drill-down, in our terminology, is required for a complexity that's contained within a larger complexity (e.g., the big data component of an overarching customer-centricity initiative). Up front we can tell our sponsors to expect to apply the Formula five times—once on the highest-level complexity, then three more times in parallel on drill-down workstreams, then a fifth time to pull all of the three workstreams together into a unified plan. What we can't tell them in advance, however, is what the three workstreams will be.

A fan-out is a repeating sequence of the application of the Formula on the same complexity in different places (e.g., across multiple regions, business units, customer segments, or product lines): dealership engagement in Region A, then Region B, then Region C; growth mind-set in the Call Center, then in Financial Services, then in Real Estate; or change-the-trajectory brand planning in Product 1, then Product 2, then Product 3.

We can't know the specifics about what drill-downs will be needed until the requisite variety group has discovered together what those are. And while we *can* know the plan for fan-outs, we won't know for sure that they're necessary or what sequence makes the most sense until the requisite variety group has done their work.

When it comes to the fan-outs, we have seen some sponsors fall into the trap of thinking that they can just take the plan that was created in Region A and apply it in Region B without having to figure it out all over again. We refer to that as a "trap" because of the nature of complexity— just because it's the right plan for A, doesn't make it the right plan for B, nor does it mean that the people working in B will believe it's the right plan and execute it (since they weren't involved in cocreating it).

Alicia

Alicia is mental health director at Micbern, a large health system in the Southwest with a network of healthcare facilities and affiliated universities. It is working to mobilize organizations and institutions throughout the state to tackle the mental health crisis.

Heading into the three days I was optimistic, but I thought that whatever solutions we came up with, it would be Micbern who would have to be the main driver of change. What surprised me the most about what emerged was that representatives from other organizations were really owning and championing various action initiatives.

In the "things to do" bucket, all representatives from health systems and hospitals decided to:

- Put together training to educate clinicians on basic mental health and substance abuse treatment to alleviate the shortage of psychiatrists, as well as similar training for hospital security, ER workers, police officers, and school teachers in local communities;
- Create metrics and mechanisms focused on improving workplace safety and emotional support for mental healthcare staff, come up with better staffing processes to prevent overwork, and examine pay disparities within health systems;
- Identify "superuser" patients who cycle in and out of psychiatric emergency rooms frequently and create cross-institutional teams that will help these patients obtain housing and access to social services and treatment clinics in order to reduce rates of readmission.

It was remarkable how many of the ideas we captured were ideas that someone else was already doing. For instance, the last idea was brought up by someone casually. She was a nurse who told a story about how she helped a patient, whom she had noticed was being admitted to the psychiatric emergency room multiple times a week, to find housing and apply for disability so that he could get the resources to get on his feet. After that, his visits to the emergency room fell off dramatically. The department heads within Micbern were excited to hear this and immediately started thinking of ways to scale her efforts.

In the "things to try" bucket, we agreed to try a few different lobbying approaches aimed at securing a state waiver of a Medicaid rule that prohibited the use of federal dollars for treatment facilities with more than 16 beds (a rule from an era in which government was trying to deinstitutionalize mental healthcare). A handful of states have already successfully obtained the waiver, and our state could be next. It would be a unified initiative including stakeholders from multiple sectors. And using whatever tactics work best, we plan to continue to lobby together on behalf of people struggling with their mental health. We also put together a committee to study the idea of creating crisis intervention centers to which police officers could divert people with behavioral health issues instead of jail or the emergency room. The center would act as "urgent care" and house people for less than 24 hours, then redirect them to longer-term facilities if needed. It would save taxpayers lots of money that is otherwise sunk into psychiatric emergency rooms or the police manpower required to drive people to emergency rooms, to admitting hospitals, and sometimes state psychiatric hospitals. A clinic in a nearby region has already offered to be a pilot crisis intervention site. Lastly, a group of large urban health systems, including Micbern, and smaller rural hospitals decided to band together to figure out ways of organizing and sharing resources to keep afloat medical services in rural areas.

As we began talking, we realized that there were complexities all over the place that we didn't have the right people in the room to fully explore and tackle, but that we still wanted to call out and highlight. For instance, after much debate about what mental illness was, how it impacted people's responsibility for the crimes they commit, and how best to handle repeat offenders in the justice system, one judge suggested that we needed at least "another three days" to do justice to that topic (chuckling at his own double entendre). And some social workers proposed that greater invest-ment in community development—job training, child care, education—to strengthen the social safety net was needed, as the data shows that suicide rates tend to increase during economic downturns.[2] The group rejected another key topic: mental health initiatives related to teens (particularly girls) on social media. People were passionate about this one but felt that a more tech savvy crowd, maybe even augmented with representatives from some of the social media platforms, would be better able to tackle it.

The public health representative from our state government volun-teered to oversee the entire plan's execution, with representatives from across the system's various stakeholder groups acting on steering com-mittees and participating in communication activities together, while also running or working on projects that contributed to the overall, coowned plan.

It took our entire group several steps with several different discussion groups on a handful of disparate workstreams to get to a new road map for our state. We kept the focus in all these workstreams on improving health outcomes, heading off debate about who was most "responsible" for the current crisis. The first day was disorienting and a little chaotic; the second day was better as we were more familiar with each other, but our ideas felt scattered and in some cases, same-old-same-old; the third day, we built genuine momentum and arrived at a refined and integrated set of actions.

Through all of it, we took the time to explain that the "we" in the question was everyone in the room, insisting that all decisions call out which of the stakeholder groups would own the action together.

I left the three days feeling that it wasn't just Micbern who was shouldering the burden of this crisis; everyone else shared ownership for it and was accountable for saving as many lives as we could.

CHAPTER 14

The Payoff

E ACH OF OUR HEROES applied the Formula from start to finish and each of their organizations achieved the intended power leap. They started by acknowledging the complexity. They anchored the effort in a really good question and convened and level-set the right group. They put the people in their groups on a deliberate collision course and made their interactions highly productive. They iterated on each agenda item, progressing on each topic while simultaneously making connections across all topics, to emerge with integrated answers to their respective questions. The Formula very quickly engaged, aligned, and mobilized a critical mass of people as they met a complex challenge.

Now let's take a look at their results.

Brenda's Payoff

We're six months down the road from the few days we spent together resetting our partnership. Before we brought everyone together, I was at best hoping for Danley-Ross to commit a bigger marketing budget and more time per week toward our joint program. I never would have dreamt that we would find a rallying point together that fit so well with the brand and with our joint value proposition for members. Sure, Plesius is still pulling a bit more weight, but for once, there's no need to explain our partnership to a Danley-Ross employee. Quite the opposite—there is now an urgency within both organizations, whereas before it felt like pulling teeth.

And our partnership—which we have now officially named Fina-Health—has expanded. Once people woke up to the clear synergy between our offerings and their community, everyone wanted in. We're not just offering financial planning; we're also offering appropriate lending and specialized credit cards just for Danley-Ross' community. The opportunity that brought us together has now multiplied, which has been great for Plesius. I'm beginning to think (based on the signs so far) that not only will we hit our 500 percent target, we're on track to do better than that—both in terms of the original program and with the extensions we're implementing.

Not only was this a real eye-opener for what we can achieve, thanks to this, we are also now exploring partnerships with other niche communities. Sky's the limit.

Pablo's Payoff

I felt this great surge and buzz of energy as we left the room. We were, for the first time in a long time, aligned on clear direction with a common understanding of the challenges and opportunities ahead. Much less finger-pointing, much more genuine collaboration, because this time everyone—from the executives to the factory floor, from the old guard to the start-ups—was involved in creating the future. There was no one else to blame if our ideas were faulty; we now felt joint ownership for them.

That energy lasted well beyond the time we had everyone together. People returned to their cubicles, factories, and open offices with stories about what happened and the robust plan we managed to create. Then as we started rolling out various initiatives, I worked hard, based on the feedback I received, to field-test my language to make sure it was connecting and resonating with people. I made clear that I was willing to weather short-term losses for the sake of long-term sustainability of the company. I backed that claim up by laying out a concrete plan, making longer-term investments and publicly setting the right expectations with investors.

To be honest, the entire leadership team didn't have to worry about going around trying to convince people. We now knew we had ambassadors located in key parts of Doregan and throughout our supply chain who would explain what we were doing and why. Whenever someone said, "What are we doing?" there was someone—a peer, not a boss—who could answer. This was particularly the case between longtime employees and the younger generation; the former began to understand the urgency and necessity of change, and the latter began to appreciate the complexity of the challenge and respect the history of our company.

What happened during those three days was an inflection point for us. Afterward, we made some big moves. Some were clearly overdue and had varying impact. Others were quite clever and innovative and allowed us to increase or, in some cases, maintain margins for several of our legacy brands at a time in which our competitors' were mostly eroding, and while we deliberately worked on our transformation. Don't get me wrong—this is a tough business. But we've gone from a red light to a yellow light almost overnight. Now my team and I have been huddling to launch into expanding and tailoring our strategy for Brazil and Asia.

Alicia's Payoff

Did we execute everything we came up with? Certainly not everything. But for the first time, we were seeing statewide progress on mental health. Collaborations between organizations that never really got along or never worked together before started to emerge. Hospitals and treatment clinics and groups were coming together to create common processes for referrals, warm handoffs, and data sharing—at Micbern, it became increasingly rare for patients to be discharged from psychiatric emergency rooms with merely a recommendation to "find a psychiatrist." Law enforcement agencies began reaching out to our medical and social work schools to get training to improve their frontline responses. One sheriff said to me, "I didn't come into this work to be a medical responder and a social worker; I came here to enforce the law and that's what I'm good at. But I'm realizing I have to be more than that if I don't want to keep dealing with the same people night in and night out." Personally, it became much easier for me to pick up the phone and call so-and-so from the state, from law enforcement, or from an insurer to make a request because we had established a relationship. Our brief time together had established a foundation of trust and catalyzed the creation of this network.

Our retention rates for mental healthcare professionals within Micbern are improving, thanks to various changes we've made in the workplace, especially in the pursuit of safety. I've also started seeing a shift in attitudes that doctors and nurses had in our health system toward mental illness and drug abuse thanks to the training programs we've rolled out, emphasizing that people with mental illness should be accorded the same respect as people with cancer, heart disease, etc. I even overheard one doctor, about whom I've received multiple complaints for his condescending attitude, tell a person who had bipolar disorder and drug addiction, "What matters is not whether you're addicted to something—I'm addicted to coffee—but whether your addiction is disruptive to your life. We can help. And I'm going to make sure you don't leave here without having the chance to talk to one of our addiction specialists." I was pleasantly surprised at his effort to destigmatize addiction and to try to relate to his patient.

There is a lot of work left to do, but for the first time in a long time, I feel hopeful and part of a joint—not solitary—effort.

Over to You

Imagine that you put a pot of water on the stove and set the temperature to "low." You wait for it to come to a boil. Five minutes. Ten minutes. After an hour, you begin to realize that it will never come to a boil. That is akin to how most people respond when they encounter a complex problem requiring thousands of high-quality collisions amongst a group of people with requisite variety, but instead choose to approach it as if it is only complicated: The metaphorical water never boils because you can't generate the necessary energy or heat fast enough.

The tried-and-true models and approaches for complicated challenges are fundamentally a mismatch for complex challenges. If there's a checklist to execute, why bother muddying the water with questions like:

- How do I frame the challenge properly?
- Who are the right people to solve it? What requisite variety needs to be involved?

- How do I engage them in solving the challenge?
- And how many collisions will I need to engineer and manage amongst them, so they can sense, absorb, and think as a group all at once, exponentially faster? 500? 1,000? 5,000? 10,000?

Like it or not, for complex challenges it really is a binary choice: one model works at pace and at scale, while the other simply can't. The hub-and-spoke model is structurally constrained to a linear process of sensing, absorbing, thinking, and deciding. It is unable to deliver the high-volume, high-quality collisions you need to solve complex challenges. And it places too much emphasis on a small group to do the solving. In contrast, when people come together in the right way to sense, absorb, think, and decide, they achieve parallel processing. You find better solutions faster, with buy-in.

You now know that solving complex challenges, mobilizing all the right players and getting to results can actually be incredibly fast. You understand that complex challenges require a different mind-set and exponential approaches. With such knowledge, there's no going back. The Formula lays out how to turn your newfound understandings into action and compresses the required time to do so down to mere days or weeks.

The Formula provides you with a powerful way to distinguish yourself within your organization and your career. In today's world, the ability to solve complicated problems has been devalued into the commonplace. It's what you're expected to do when you come to the workplace. So, how do you develop a name and a reputation for yourself? Master the process for solving complex problems:

- Learn how to quickly identify and scope complex problems.
- Frame questions effectively.
- Assemble the right team to address the challenge and equip them to work together effectively.
- Create many, many high-value interactions amongst them—and do that fast.

When you lead an initiative to solve a complex problem and apply the Formula, people will notice that you produced results quickly. You'll become a "go to" person when other complex challenges (or opportunities) arise. Depending on where you are in your career, you may not have the convening authority to tackle a complex challenge that requires 10,000 collisions. That's okay. Start with a smaller, but still complex, challenge. You might be able to convene a group to tackle a challenge that requires 500 or 1,000 collisions. Use the Formula to help you crack complexity, and your reputation and capability will grow.

The bar has been set. Hold fast to what we've laid out for you here and make it your prevailing mind-set. It is the requisite mind-set. Let it permeate everything you do every time you power up to solve something important. Apply it to the biggest challenges you face; have it also inform the way in which you manage your everyday, usual interactions and small group meetings. To meet both of these goals, keep asking yourself these questions:

- What kind of challenge are we facing? Is it complex or merely complicated?

- Am I using every opportunity to drive shared understanding about the challenge? Am I framing it properly? Do I have others' agreement on the problem statement?

- Am I involving the right people—the sensors, absorbers, thinkers, deciders, and actors? How will I engage them? What outside voices, what other perspectives, and what other personalities will they need to round out their variety?

- How can I level-set them? With respect to the data, information, and knowledge they collectively have access to, what's important and what's just noise? What else do they need?

- How can I help them decipher their specialized and localized dialects and codes and concepts that usually impede shared understanding?

- How can I ensure that the individuals in the group feel a sense of ownership for finding and executing the right solution? What steps must I take to change the normal mode in which they engage with each other? How do I get them out of their usual behaviors (the unproductive ones)? How do I get them to let go of their personal agendas and co-create the right one for the organization?

- How do I connect all of them together and activate those connections repeatedly, force collisions, and make sure the resulting breakthroughs (big and small) are captured?

- How do I make sure people speak their minds and listen actively? How do I bring creative tension into the interactions to ensure we're not deceiving ourselves? How will I ensure we explore, connect the dots, and translate intent into action?

The big 10,000-collision challenges often require you to follow the Formula methodically, step-by-step, if you want to crack them. However, you don't need to wait for a massively complex challenge. You can put the ideas to work to help you solve smaller—more everyday—complex challenges. Here are a few ways to get started, perhaps as soon as your next meeting:

- Great questions and high-variety groups make meetings better in general. The critic role creates healthy tension and forces behavior change when people are talking together about anything substantive. Iteration gives people time to let go and to put pieces together.

- The notion of requisite variety—the zones and the other characteristics—applies always; project teams, executive teams, boards, councils, think tanks—all benefit from a purposeful application of Ashby's Law: "Only variety destroys variety."

- Paying attention to the cost of codification will provide a significant return on investment, saving you and your people / teams from unnecessary churn, confusion, false starts, and false consensus. Anytime two or more people are discussing anything—ask yourself (and them) if they are speaking the same language. Encourage them to take the time (e.g., by adding an extra meeting or going out for dinner together) to talk about the way things *are* before talking about the way they *should be*—the 'it is' conversation will reveal many of the lurking language barriers.

- The right agenda matters, and when you're going into a meeting (or a series of meetings or a series of interactive sessions of any kind) it is worth taking the time to co-create the agenda with the group. Otherwise, you risk covering only what matters to you, not what matters to the group. Worse, you risk leaving off the agenda essential topics that aren't even on your radar. Schedules impose discipline and respect people's time—set a schedule; but don't confuse that with an agenda.

- Collisions create value. Driving people into contact with each other in new and creative ways at unusual times with or without context—that's how serendipity happens. Innovation centers and forward-thinking organizations incorporate collision design into their physical spaces. You can go them one better by intentionally overlapping team rosters, steering committee membership, meeting invitees, etc.

Become a proponent for this approach to complexity. Spread the word about cracking the code. Be a role model who shows the way. You now see and understand something fundamental that others do not, yet. You possess the vision and the tools to capitalize on this Formula—a Formula that is increasingly critical in an increasingly complex society.

Various forces are placing unprecedented pressure on most organizations and societies, and the knee-jerk reaction is leaders doubling down on higher and higher performance expectations of their people and partners. The linear model of progress has been your model for decades, which means you've been conditioned to expect a slow trajectory toward results, notwithstanding pleas to go faster.

Don't fall into the trap into which you've been conditioned to stumble. When you ask people to devote a couple of days to what you know can be a power leap, many will tell you they're too busy to give you that much time. Don't let that resistance veer you off course; don't fall back into accepting a plodding preplanned trajectory with regular status meetings and gates and so on. Don't give in. This is where you must evangelize. Now, you're aware of what's possible. It's your opportunity and your responsibility as a leader to show the way.

Act, and this will quickly become what you're known for, what people reference when they talk about your strengths. You will become a master of orchestrating rapid progress in the face of complexity.

It is akin to becoming the best of conductors, but under extreme circumstances: conducting orchestras made up of musicians of varying abilities; playing without sheet music; performing pieces you and they haven't ever heard or played before, in front of a fickle and anxious audience with very high expectations; where only a peak performance, every time, will cut muster.

When you and your special-purpose group achieve peak performance, you co-create something special together. Everyone—you, the players, your customers, and stakeholders—all know that something special has been created, something memorable, something with distinct impact, something that will have longevity.

When you've mastered the Formula, it opens up possibilities that you couldn't previously seize. Now that you can achieve power leaps on demand by being able to sense-absorb-think-decide-and-act at an exponential pace, you can tackle your biggest and your most important challenges much faster and more effectively than ever before.

Complexity isn't a temporary, transitional thing. It's a type of challenge that we've been encountering since we first rose to our feet and tried out our opposable thumbs, and will continue to encounter long after we've left this planet for new horizons.

In fact, complexity is going to continue to deepen and widen in the coming years, and organizations lacking the Formula will become increasingly unable to keep up, vulnerable to competitors who "get it," just like organizations who ignored digitization to their later (and present) peril.

As we've said already, "getting it" may entail using all the steps in the Formula or simply beginning with its basic principles as guidance when dealing with complex issues.

If you want to crack complexity, you need the code. This book provides that code and how to use it. It's not science fiction, it's not something to eagerly anticipate. You can start using it immediately to rapidly accelerate progress—take leaps—on all the complexities you and your organization are facing.

There's so much to do and so much time and talent to do it. It's just a matter of deciding which challenge opportunity to get after next.

So, over to you. . .

Where Else?

W ITH SOME EXPERIENCE, you won't just use the Formula to *react* to complexities. Instead, you'll proactively spot and pursue opportunities that are emerging out of the increasingly complex world: bitcoin, blockchain, urbanization, AI/machine learning, disintermediation, and so on. How could you seize advantage in your industry on some of those things? What else is coming and how could you get in front of those developments?

The next few pages will help you think about where else you could be applying the Formula and should stretch your thinking beyond the obvious one or two challenges that come immediately to mind. What are the possibilities for you? Start by reflecting on what others are already doing with the Formula.

Where Organizations Are Applying the Formula

Growth in South America

One multinational used a power leap to double the growth of one of its businesses in South America. They wanted to double growth in two ways—organic in-segment growth and through the introduction of new products and technologies from two of its other businesses. The local team was very talented, the market was growing rapidly, the company had high-quality products, the local leadership team was mixed with up-and-coming leaders from headquarters and was supported by the global team. Workshops and training had been held. Consultants had been in. Something wasn't clicking. They were stuck. HQ knew it. The South American team knew it. Previous attempts weren't resulting in the kind of mind-set and action required to change the trajectory.

Using the Formula, they co-created a cross-division plan, and the South American team took ownership of it. They saw immediate traction turn into sustained focus and change, new levels of collaboration between businesses, and growth within the first few pilot accounts.

Grow Faster than the Industry

The CEO of a Fortune 500 company was intent on growing faster than the rest of the industry. The company's sales were in decline, and this needed to be reversed. The company was losing relevance with consumers, yet efforts to gain relevance by introducing seemingly beneficial changes to some of their products were causing backlash from the bulk of their consumer base. Big, confusing issues like Amazon, e-commerce, and channel convergence were going unresolved. Young employees—who seemed to expect their employer to be an extension of their personal values—were putting a new kind of pressure on the business. Business units were autonomous and decentralized. Leadership was having a hard time prioritizing, knowing that the organization had no excess capacity.

With one powerful leap, the company got at the essence of the internal barriers to change. They used the leap to quickly reorganize in a way that truly resonated with employees and their markets.

Disrupt Ourselves

The executive team and board of a financial services organization were well aware of how other agent-based industries (like travel and real estate) had been disrupted as the internet brought customers direct access to services that had previously required an intermediary. Having experienced leaps before in risk management and on value proposition, they decided they needed rapid acceleration on envisioning possible futures, understanding potential disruptors, and "blue-skying" their own possible responses.

In one leap, the leadership team, together with several future leaders of the organization and some outside help, explored the future as if they were a start-up entering the industry with no legacy holding them back from making the right choices. They emerged with both a short-term plan to gain market share in the current business model while simultaneously readying themselves for impending disruption.

Create New Digital Businesses

A conglomerate with several existing digital businesses at various stages of maturity was intent on seizing $3 billion in new profit by looking across their existing digital ecosystem to find new business opportunities. The chair and the CEO both saw this as an opportunity that was fast becoming a necessity—new, powerful competitors were beginning to enter their markets, and consumer preferences and behavior were changing. Given their scope and scale, they had a bona fide window of opportunity to create an even stickier, self-reinforcing ecosystem that consumers would love, and at the same time seize a dominant position in several traditional markets. If they continued to hesitate by not figuring it out and aligning on timing and investment, they would find themselves severely challenged by nontraditional competitors.

Other complex challenges where organizations apply the Formula include:

- Bring a whole new class of medicines to market
- Turn around a business unit with flat growth
- Bring a state up the ladder of health indices and outcomes
- Create the innovation agenda
- Create a new brand promise with proof points
- Double growth rate
- Develop talent strategy
- Make emergency readiness plans in preparation for a global influenza pandemic

- Formulate policy and mobilize stakeholders in the context of mental health and addictions, HIV/AIDS, childhood obesity, and sexual assault in the workplace
- Institutionalize enterprise key account management
- Navigate the choppy waters of postmerger integration
- Develop a national sales plan of action to overachieve on fourth-quarter quota
- Design and launch a joint venture
- Bring the organization's enterprise risk management strategy to life
- Triple earnings before interest, taxes, depreciation, and amoritization (EBITDA) in private-equity portfolio companies
- Determine and align the organization around its big data strategy
- Comply with new legislation that impacts the customer experience
- Take out cost, whether $50 million or $1.5 billion, sustainably
- Monetize dormant IP

Use this list to reflect on where else the Formula in this book could provide an important leap for you.

For organizations that experience these and other leaps, the Complexity Formula becomes an integral part of their operating system, applied to distinct challenges as needed. Many bake the Formula into cyclical business processes like strategic planning or brand planning. Doing so works best when it's not the default, but rather the way they do those things at the times when the stakes are highest.

The Leap Economy

We are already witnessing a steep decline in satisfaction with the traditional way in which organizations seek to find clarity and mobilize in the face of complexity. The next few years will bring an increasing number of alternatives to the market. Large and boutique traditional consulting firms will continue to thrive where organizations are most comfortable and can afford to move at the traditional pace with the traditional expenditure. They will also continue to become increasingly embedded in the implementation work.

Some of these firms, along with newer alternatives, will innovate services, products, and platforms that help their clients take leaps drawing mainly on their own talent and the talent of stakeholders in their ecosystem but augmented by experts who specialize as "requisite-variety-for-hire."

We call this the Leap Economy, and it will be characterized by and benefit from many of the insights, capabilities, services, and technologies we reflected on throughout the book:

- A rapidly changing, highly complex environment where only tireless "hares" thrive;
- Mainstream recognition that requisite variety large groups and many-to-many networks trump expert-based hub-and-spoke approaches;
- A strong belief that talent is abundant, with a sharp focus on helping organizations quickly activate the previously latent talent in and around their ecosystem to solve their biggest challenges, instead of doing the solving for them;
- The rise to mainstream of fast (just enough) research to provide baseline data-information-knowledge for groups convened for a leap;
- More advanced integration of sophisticated big-data insights with groups convened for a leap;
- A global pool of (relatively) egoless experts-for-hire, who travel around from group to group and situation to situation offering highly effective and timely expertise on whatever they specialize in (whether vertical, horizontal, or both);
- Greatly enhanced for-hire or in-house capability around experimentation design management, monitoring, and evaluation;
- Virtual and physical war rooms where leaders convene to assess and make decisions about their system's progress on their complexity agenda;

- A clear understanding of leadership as orchestration and *how* to orchestrate—rather than command-and-control.

Leaping into Other Industries

The ability to scale abundant talent to make leaps is breaking conventional models. It will change the paradigm for industries and sectors with a scarcity-based model: management consulting, research organizations, entertainment, etc. It will also give a boost to sectors struggling in the scarcity paradigm: governments, medium- to large-size businesses, multinationals, large NGOs, foundations, associations, etc.

A universal truth is that one person's complexity is another person's opportunity. Power leaps, enabled by the scaling of an abundance of talent, make these opportunities realizable. The complexity that would otherwise break the back of an organization will become that organization's opportunity to leap past the competition; or, if handled the traditional way, it will give others that opportunity.

We've discussed a variety of organizations and industries that have benefited from the Formula, but here we'd like to focus on a few industries that should be very worried about falling behind or excited at the prospect of transforming completely to leap ahead.

Management Consulting

The management consulting industry is predicated on a talent-is-scarce model, whereby the scarce talent is employed by the consulting firm and is brought to bear on clients' complex challenges. The role of the management consultant will shift from outsourced provider of solutions to participant in power leaps as well as the downstream systems-integration work they have become increasingly involved in. The need for solving complex challenges has not diminished, but the appetite for the old model has shrunk.

The need to solve the complex not only remains but intensifies and spreads. Power leaps will solve the management consulting shortfall—rapid, smart decisions in the face of complexity with coordinated action built in to the solution.

Sport

A sports team can gain significant advantage by applying the Complexity Formula to its on-field tactics and player acquisition/development strategies. These strategies are currently the product of the team's intelligentsia, carefully developed and controlled by presidents of sports operations, general managers, and head coaches (and maybe a few others).

Sports teams' growing reliance on data is ratcheting up the complexity and thus creating an increasingly compelling scenario for the Formula.

Teams will be able to blow the doors off their current strategic planning processes by embracing requisite variety and cocreation. Imagine having the senior leadership, players, field coaches, and equipment managers aligned from the start on what the team is doing to win: how they will innovate on the field; how they will make better draft selections and develop young talent; how they will make the team more attractive to free agents; how they will involve players in the community to drive stronger grassroots support; and so on.

Marketing Services / Advertising Agencies

Marketing and advertising are domains that, again, have traditionally relied on Don Draper–like talent to do the heavy lifting on creative concepts, campaign design, slogans, and messaging. We've been working in this space for years.

In many of our customer organizations, marketing teams regularly apply the Complexity Formula to genuinely engage large, cross-functional groups in marketing development. They get great answers *and* unprecedented alignment and buy-in from support functions and sales, which leads to success in execution.

Increasingly, rather than going to top agencies to do the groundbreaking creative development, organizations can leverage requisite variety (augmented by one or two stars from their agency partners) to deliver the goods much faster and more effectively.

In that vein, we've tried a few things as well: one marketing firm used a power leap to fine-tune a key pitch that the team wasn't aligned on, five days before the presentation. A major retailer used a power leap to choose between a handful of campaign concepts quickly produced by a top agency, validate and flesh out that campaign, and produce great ideas for supporting tactics. The participating agency was amazed by the speed and quality of the result.

Books, Music, and Graphic Arts

Creative pursuits have traditionally been the protected domain of the artist. Books get written by authors, or sometimes by coauthors. New music is created by one or two inspired individuals. Dance, graphic art, theatre . . . solo pursuits.

All of these domains could benefit from the application of the Complexity Formula.

We're not saying that a requisite variety group can write a book together, or paint a picture, or choreograph a dance, or compose music. We are saying, however, that at some point in these creative endeavors, there's potentially massive benefit to be had from the accelerated involvement of all the right people. For example, convening a large group of people to review a draft manuscript (as we did on the book you're reading), or convening a song-writing megajam that offers diverse musicians and lyricists the opportunity to collaborate on their projects, or bringing an arts community together to talk about how they can collectively inspire and be inspired by the talent and patrons amongst and around them.

Research-Based Organizations

The Complexity Formula could facilitate certain kinds of research (as an alternative to surveys, for example). Some life sciences and ICT companies, along with major NGOs and global associations, have been doing this with us for years when they apply the Complexity Formula to running advisory boards.

But here we mean something much more ambitious—getting at core research (in the pharmaceutical space, for example, this would be drug development). Think about engineering serendipitous breakthroughs in medicine or other research domains. Or many domains at once.

Assuming researchers are willing to share a little more openly than they've done in the past, we believe that bringing researchers together from within one domain (e.g., lung cancer) or across multiple domains (e.g., all cancers, or medicine, rocket science, artificial intelligence, and so on) would spark significant breakthroughs.

If you pick a specific research-based industry, like pharmaceuticals again, we know that a key challenge they face comes downstream from drug discovery, when it's time to commercialize what's been developed in the laboratories. What if they involved the commercial teams—and in the case of pharma, market access and regulatory teams—right from the start of the research process? They could help point researchers at the specific challenges they know the market is dealing with, patient challenges, physician issues with traditional therapies, and pharmacoeconomic arguments that payers are looking for. Imagine the increased efficiency if the entire enterprise is aligned at the start on what needs to be coming out of the pipeline, years before it will bear fruit.

Ecosystems and Joint Ventures

As governments become increasingly insular and pull back from funding international aid (for example), a financial and leadership void is being created that will need to be filled through private-public partnerships. The Complexity Formula is a platform for the formation of, strategy-setting for, and ongoing coordination of joint efforts among organizations.

Entire ecosystems that are collaborating for the common good (e.g., multiple business organizations in partnership to deliver a promising value proposition that none could realize alone) use the Formula and the leaps it produces to accelerate and improve on the impact they have.

Private Equity

Private-equity firms already use the Formula to help their portfolio companies advance more rapidly. These firms are increasingly using the Formula to differentiate themselves for increasingly picky institutional investors, make better investments, and accelerate returns with more consistency and far less cost and effort.

Incubators

Incubators can apply the Complexity Formula to bring together the entrepreneurs they are seeding with each other and with the network of mentors and coaches and support service organizations (law, finance, etc.) that surround them. The opportunities for engineered serendipity, learning, and collaborations will increase the likelihood and pace of success for the portfolio of companies being incubated.

Personal Complexity

Here's a final thought on interesting applications of the Formula: Complexity isn't limited to organizations, systems, or ecosystems. Individuals face personal complexity all the time and reach turning points in their life when complexity is overwhelming and personal stakes are at their highest. Examples include: Choosing where to live one's life after graduation; restarting a stagnant career; starting a family; dealing with aging parents or personal health challenges; planning a milestone anniversary.

The Complexity Formula can be applied on these and all other personal complexities. Articulate the question, identify requisite variety (family members, coach/mentor, favorite university professor, friends, religious leaders, and total strangers), and then work with them to find your answers by applying the rest of the steps.

APPENDIX **B**

Troubleshooting

Overcoming Obstacles, Correcting Mistakes

What can go wrong?

This may seem too good to be true, since if you're a veteran leader, you've witnessed all types of management fads and theories that didn't pan out. As much as you resonate with our approach to complexity, you may be hearing a voice in your head asking, "What's the catch?"

There is no catch.

That said, if you're like most of the companies and organizations we've worked with, there are certainly some barriers to watch out for.

In the following tables, we've summarized our experiences and our customers' experiences using the same 10-step structure that you're now familiar with. We've mentioned a few of these barriers already along the way and we'll repeat some advice we've already offered, but by putting it in this form, we hope to provide a tool you can use quickly and easily if you encounter problems: A troubleshooting guide for each step, if you will.

Step-by-Step Troubleshooting

Step 1. Acknowledge the complexity

The basic task here is to recognize that you're facing complexity, that you don't know what you don't know, and that you're going to need to approach things differently than you have in the past.

Barrier	Symptom	Impact	Response
Senior leadership denial / the immune system of the organization	Senior leadership and other influencers passively or actively resisting your efforts	Paralysis, delays and roadblocks creating time lags you can't afford, people not engaging	Find something 'safe' on which to apply the Formula a first time and prove its value.
Loyalty to traditional approaches and the partners who deploy them			Invite those partners in to your requisite variety.
Pride / control issues	Discomfort admitting to a seeming inadequacy to solve the problem, and/or with letting go of the reins	Hesitancy to engage with the requisite variety group and hand the challenge over to them	Remain the champion, join the requisite variety, and demonstrate that you know how to solve for complexity.

Step 2. Construct a really, really good question

Here, you need to identify what system you're dealing with, what the complexity is, what the goals and time lines should be, and how to put all of that into a really compelling question.

Barrier	Symptom	Impact	Response
The system facing the challenge is ill-defined and unowned; or owned but not yours.	No personal authority to get after the challenge; no single owner who has the authority	Need to build consensus amongst several groups slows things down; no single source for funding	Step up to the funding if the ROI for your organization is big; take the lead / initiative in selling the Formula to others and getting their support; use the question as a selling tool and commit your own people first.
The system isn't interested in solving the challenge.	No uptake on talk of solving it; heads in the sand about the threat	Time delay, failure to get commitments from people, no traction	Make the case for the value of solving the challenge (express it in $s if you can).

Barrier	Symptom	Impact	Response
The complexity defies definition; it's too big or too nebulous.	No amount of question-writing is adequately expressing the complexity.	Can't come up with a good question	Choose one "deck" from which to jump into the complexity (e.g., talent strategy) or come up with a question that you know can't be answered without addressing the complexity (e.g., growth).
The question seems to be the wrong question.	Everyone is getting hung up on the question.	People aren't solving the challenge, just arguing about the question.	Be open to changing it, but beware of watering it down, introducing bias, or skirting the main issue in doing so.

Step 3. Target a requisite variety of solvers

The success of the Complexity Formula relies heavily on the involvement of requisite variety. In this step, the job is to get them to give you their time and focus.

Barrier	Symptom	Impact	Response
Requisite variety represents too many people.	The invitee list has 50+ names on it.	Can't deal with that number of people in one session; can't afford to convene them all	Reduce the scope of the challenge or break the application of the Formula into several steps (e.g., starting with senior leaders, then later with the 'doers').
No convening power for requisite variety	Can't make people come, can only ask them to	Everyone needs to be convinced, and too many can just say no.	Go up the chain to find a champion with convening power—sell that person first, then get their name on the invitation.

Barrier	Symptom	Impact	Response
Can't realistically involve requisite variety (e.g., your customers)	It's too risky to 'open the kimono' with outsiders, with lower levels of the organization, etc.	Can't really achieve requisite variety and thus the best possible result	Use proxies who are closest to the groups you can't involve; be explicit that they are to represent those groups.
Key people are resisting or unavailable.	Important people are declining to engage.	Missing key voices	Stress their individual importance, stroke their egos, ask for alternative times when they would be willing to join, and reschedule if necessary.
Key perspectives / people are excluded or forgotten.	People point out their absence from the group.	Missing key voices and the opportunity for key engagement	Involve them in the steps that will come later (e.g., vetting the action plan, serving on the steering committee, solving subsequent complexities).

Step 4. Localize the solvers

Getting people together is the imperative here.

Barrier	Symptom	Impact	Response
People won't come or won't stay.	"I can't be there the whole time," "Can I join remotely?," "Can I send a delegate?"	Missing key voices (if they don't come) or missing their necessary focus	Ensure the objection is really about availability (and not resistance) and find the next best substitute, but don't let them choose a delegate because they might not be the right person.
People don't want to (or shouldn't) be in the same room together.	Everyone knows that those two people together will ruin the experience / outcomes for everyone else.	They may be disruptive in the beginning, but the group itself will ultimately drown out the noise they make; the impact of *not* bringing them together is potentially more severe since they are part of the complexity.	Bring them together, coach them ahead of time, then have them colliding with each other and with everyone else as equals; they will marvel after about the common ground they share.

Step 5. Eliminate the noise

You're trying to help people cut through the noise, but that's hard to do when there's so much noise and you can't necessarily separate what matters from what doesn't.

Barrier	Symptom	Impact	Response
Missing key data/ information	Unable to or failed to source key data / information (e.g., current customer satisfaction numbers)	People believe they can't do what they're being asked to do without the data.	Ask the group to rely on their tacit knowledge, state their assumptions, and/or fill in the blanks with at-hand data as people realize they need it.
People can't agree on even the most basic facts.	Discussions are at a standstill as people argue the facts.	Slow progress, frustration, disengagement	Call a time-out and get everyone together to remedy the situation (e.g., by getting the facts straight, by getting better data, by agreeing to disagree and stating some assumptions to proceed with).
The data / information shared is flawed and/or biased.	People are disputing the data / information instead of talking about the challenge.		

Step 6. Agree on the right agenda

Your requisite variety group sets their own agenda (within the confines of the question you're asking them), and who knows what they'll come up with?

Barrier	Symptom	Impact	Response
The agenda isn't what you wanted. A key topic is missing.	A strong feeling that something is missing from the agenda and/or that something on the agenda will be a waste of time and energy	Very likely, no impact	Leave it be—the group now owns the agenda and to force a change on them is disempowering; trust that everything is there or missing for good reason and that there will be opportunities to address either case along the way (e.g., redirecting a topic, adding a missing topic into another related one).
There is insufficient expertise amongst the people in the overall group to do justice to a key topic.	A topic seems important but there's nobody in the room who knows enough about it.	The topic doesn't get proper coverage, and people become frustrated / disillusioned about the progress they can make as a result.	Shape the topic so that the group can handle it without the experts and agree that there will be some guessing and assumptions that will need to be validated later, or take the topic out of scope for now and treat it as a TBD.

Barrier	Symptom	Impact	Response
People can't agree on the topics.	The agenda-setting comes to a grinding halt.	An agenda is needed to move on, so progress stops until there is resolution.	Keep shaping and reshaping topics during the agenda-setting until you can find consensus; ultimately, call it to a vote.
A taboo topic is key (e.g., leadership, physician payment models, dealing with poor performers).	People agree that a topic is important, but people are generally skittish about discussing it.	Something important gets left behind, potentially undermining the entire exercise.	Face the topic head-on and assure everyone it's okay to discuss it; sign up for it yourself and demonstrate what it means to be open to discussing it.

Step 7. Put people on a collision course

It's one thing to say you need a many-to-many network model and forced collisions, it's another to do that well.

Barrier	Symptom	Impact	Response
You don't know how to set up a many-to-many network.	Temptation to just throw people together and hope the right things happen	No guarantee of the collisions you need, or good collisions	Focus on using meetings on the identified topics as the formal settings for collisions; keep the groups small in those meetings (5–8 people talking at a time) so the collisions are meaningful; assign people into those meetings to optimize how many others they overlap with.
People aren't happy with their place in the network.	"Why am I in that topic? I don't know anything about that," and/or "How can I *not* be in that topic, I'm very close to it."	Unless they're absence means a lack of key expertise, or their presence is genuinely a problem, very little impact. The more important impact is potential disengagement or passive resistance.	People learn a lot from attending topics they don't know much about and contribute in surprising ways. If people who are usually involved in a topic miss it this time, you can expect completely new ideas and outcomes. The connections between topics amount to everyone contributing to every topic, directly or indirectly.

Barrier	Symptom	Impact	Response
The sequence of topics doesn't seem to make sense.	"How can we talk about x if we haven't first talked about y?"	None—sequence doesn't matter.	This isn't a linear, step-by-step examination of the topics; it's nonlinear and sequence never matters in retrospect.

Step 8. Advance iteratively and emergently

Iteration and emergence will get you there, but it requires some patience.

Barrier	Symptom	Impact	Response
People want to solve first and rationalize later.	In Iteration 1, frustration that the group is being held back from answering the question and instead encouraged to have a gripe session	If people don't talk status quo first, they don't share baseline information, stories, issues, and so on that will be key to the group finding the right answers.	Hold people to the task of using the first iteration to share information, even if they don't like it.

Barrier	Symptom	Impact	Response
People think two iterations is enough.	"We're done. No need for a third iteration?"	Missing the third iteration means missing all the convergence, retracing of steps, challenging of assumptions, processing of new information, etc., that come with it. The impact is having partial and potentially wrong clarity on what needs to be done.	The third iteration is always profoundly important, so push people through their misguided belief that it's not necessary— they will thank you when it's over.

Step 9. Change how people interact

What happens in collision teams, with just the right number of people present for effective conversations, is what drives the progress made across all the topics on the overarching question; those meetings have to be really good, and we've given you some strong guidance on how to make them so.

Barrier	Symptom	Impact	Response
People won't play along with their roles.	Outbursts, people talking when they should be listening, and vice versa	Too many people talking at once, disorder, bad meeting	Apologize in advance for holding people to their roles, then enforce them politely but firmly.
People aren't respecting the clock.	People are arriving late, meetings aren't starting on time, and some meetings are getting less time than they should.	Diminishing faith in 'the process,' less camaraderie, imbalance in time afforded teams to have important discussions	Show right from the start that time matters. Start on time even if some key people are missing, start meetings on time, end them on time, and keep reminding people where they need to be and when. The sponsoring team needs to be modeling the desired behavior throughout.

Step 10. Translate clarity and insights into action

By the end, you and your requisite variety group have clarity on what needs to happen. For some, that may be where the really hard work begins.

Barrier	Symptom	Impact	Response
We aren't good at follow-through.	People are saying at the end, "Great session, but the proof will be in whether or not we follow through *this* time."	Complexity doesn't get solved if there's not execution.	Set up proper governance; use your requisite variety group within the governance structure to keep you honest and on track.
We aren't good at running or monitoring experiments.	Pilots and prototypes never end, and everybody knows that.	In the complex domain you try things, you amplify what works and stop what doesn't. If you're not doing that, meaningful progress is severely hampered.	Acquire outside help.

Barrier	Symptom	Impact	Response
We can't do everything that surfaced.	People are overwhelmed by the sheer volume of actions that were identified—all of which seem important.	Usually much, but not all needs to be done, and sequence, timing, who's doing it, etc., go a long way to making the work manageable. If it's all treated as one massive effort, then people won't execute, and the complexity won't be dealt with.	Do a planning exercise to agree on priorities, sequence, and interdependencies. Find 3 areas to focus on that cover most of everything else.

Endnotes

Chapter 1—Journey into the Unknown

1. Alvin Toffler, *Future Shock* (New York: Bantam Books, 1971), 2.
2. Stafford Beer, *Platform for Change* (Chichester: Wiley, 1975), 18.
3. John German, "History," Santa Fe Institute, https://www.santafe.edu/about/history.
4. John Holland, *Complexity: A Very Short Introduction* (New York: Oxford University Press: 2014).
5. Maggie Fox, "Suicide rates are up 30 percent since 1999, CDC says," *NBC News*, Health, June 7, 2018, https://www.nbcnews.com/health/health-news/suicide-rates-are-30-percent-1999-cdc-says-n880926.
6. Maggie Fox, "Depression Worsening in Teens, Especially Girls," *NBC News*, Health, November 14, 2016, https://www.nbcnews.com/better/wellness/depression-worsening-teens-especially-girls-n683716.
7. Ana Swanson, "A shocking number of mentally ill Americans end up in prison instead of treatment," *Washington Post*, Wonkblog, April 30, 2015, https://www.washingtonpost.com/news/wonk/wp/2015/04/30/a-shocking-number-of-mentally-ill-americans-end-up-in-prisons-instead-of-psychiatric-hospitals.
8. T R. Insel, "Assessing the Economic Costs of Serious Mental Illness," *American Journal of Psychiatry* (June 2008), 165(6), 663–665.
9. David Levine, "What's the Answer to the Shortage of Mental Health Providers?", *U.S. News*, Health Care, May 25, 2018, https://

health.usnews.com/health-care/patient-advice/articles/2018-05-25/whats-the-answer-to-the-shortage-of-mental-health-care-providers.

10. "Complex," *Online Etymological Dictionary*, https://www.etymonline.com/word/complex.

Chapter 2—Getting Started

1. Russell Ackoff, *Re-creating the Corporation: A Design of Organizations for the 21st Century* (New York: Oxford University Press, 1999), 159.

2. Clay Shirky, "Does the Internet Make You Smarter?" *Wall Street Journal*, June 4, 2010, https://www.wsj.com/articles/SB10001424052748704025304575284973472694334.

Chapter 7—Step 4. Localize the Solvers

1. Aristotle and C. D. C. Reeves, *Politics: A New Translation* (Cambridge: Hackett Publishing Company, Inc., 2017), 12.

2. Daniel Goleman, *Social Intelligence: The New Science of Human Relationships* (Bantam: 2006), 4.

3. "The Meetology Laboratory 2012: Behavioural Research Results," Meetology Group (February 2014).

4. Akshata Marain, "Are face-to-face teams more creative than virtual teams?" Northwestern School of Education and Social Policy (March 2014).

5. Jing Jiang et al., "Neural Synchronization during Face-to-Face Communication," *Journal of Neuroscience* (November 2012).

6. Charles Duhigg, "What Google Learned from Its Quest to Build the Perfect Team," *New York Times Magazine*, February 25, 2016.

7. Allan and Barbara Pease, "The Definitive Book of Body Language," *New York Times*, Books, September 24, 2006, https://www.nytimes.com/2006/09/24/books/chapters/0924-1st-peas.html.

Chapter 8—Step 5. Eliminate the Noise

1. Robin Lloyd, "Metric mishap caused loss of NASA orbiter," *CNN*, Sci-Tech, September 30, 1999, http://edition.cnn.com/TECH/space/9909/30/mars.metric.02/.

2. This story is fictional, but much of it is drawn from another fictional story presented in this report: Debra A. Pinals and Doris A. Fuller, "Beyond Beds: The Vital Role of a Full Continuum of Psychiatric Care," Treatment Advocacy Center and National Association of State Mental Health Program Directors (October 2017).

3. German Lopez, "How America's criminal justice system became the country's mental health system," *Vox*, October 18, 2016, https://www.vox.com/2016/3/1/11134908/criminal-justice-mental-health.

Chapter 9—Step 6. Agree on the Right Agenda

1. Stafford Beer, "Tape 9: Syntegration," Falcondale Collection, Liverpool John Moores University, 1994, http://opendata.ljmu.ac.uk/6/23/SBFCSession09TheSyntegration.mp4.

2. C. Otto Scharmer and Katrin Kaufer, *Leading from the Emerging Future: From Ego-System to Eco-System Economies* (California: Berrett-Koehler, 2013), 21.

Chapter 10—Step 7. Put People on a Collision Course

1. David Scharfenberg, "MIT's Zuckerman on Building a More Cosmopolitan Internet," WBUR 90.9, July 17, 2013, http://www.wbur.org/news/2013/07/17/zuckerman-rewire-interview.

2. Tamar Lewin, "After setbacks, online courses are rethought," *New York Times*, December 10, 2013, http://www.nytimes.com/2013/12/11/us/after-setbacks-online-courses-are-rethought.html.

3. David Perkins, *The Eureka Effect: The Art and Logic of Breakthrough Thinking* (W. W. Norton & Company, 2001), 51–53.

Chapter 12—Step 9. Change How People Interact

1. C. Otto Scharmer and Katrin Kaufer, *Leading from the Emerging Future* (California: Berrett-Koehler Publishers, 2013), Introduction.

2. Monica Anderson and Andrew Perrin, "Technology use among seniors," Pew Research Center, Internet & Technology, May 17, 2017, http://www.pewinternet.org/2017/05/17/technology-use-among-seniors/.

Chapter 13—Step 10. Translate Clarity and Insights into Action

1. Tom Peters, "The Best Corporate Strategy? None, of Course," *Chicago Tribune*, Business, July 11, 1994, http://articles.chicagotribune.com/1994-07-11/business/9407110026_1_silicon-graphics-customers-richard-branson.

2. Maggie Fox, "Suicide rates are up 30 percent since 1999, CDC says," *NBC News*, Health, June 7, 2018, https://www.nbcnews.com/health/health-news/suicide-rates-are-30-percent-1999-cdc-says-n880926.

Index

A

abundance, 21, 28–29, 35, 204
ACT-LEAP-ACT, 33, 38–39
actual variety, 138
advertising agencies, 205
agenda setting, 119–121
agent-based industries, 200
alignment, 157, 182, 205
allies, 72
Amazon, 3, 9, 26, 33, 114, 179, 200
Ashby, W. Ross, 24
Ashby's Law, 24–25, 70, 196
attitude, 71–72, 76, 120, 193
authority, 72, 95–96, 195
autostereograms, 151–153

B

Beer, Stafford, 2
Big data, 203
books, 206
brainstorming, 120
brand promise, 201

breakthrough, 149–151
buy-in, 30, 182, 194, 205

C

channel convergence, 200
13 characteristic cross-checks, 72, 75–76
clarity, 13, 37–38, 41, 52, 62, 101, 133, 141, 148, 151, 153–154, 157, 161, 169, 177–179, 182, 184–185, 202, 223
clustering, 120
co-create, 22, 34, 183, 195–196, 198, 200
co-created agenda, 166
collaboration, 200
collision equation, 131–132
collisions, 158
collision teams, 169
common mistakes, 84–87
communication, 183–185
complex challenges, 15–16, 19, 22–24, 27, 32, 95, 133, 171, 173, 193–196, 201, 204